The Challenge of
CELL CHURCH

Text copyright © Phil Potter 2001
The author asserts the moral right
to be identified as the author of this work

Published by
The Bible Reading Fellowship
First Floor, Elsfield Hall
15–17 Elsfield Way, Oxford OX2 8FG
ISBN 1 84101 218 1

First published 2001
10 9 8 7 6 5 4 3 2 1
All rights reserved

A catalogue record for this book is available from the British Library

Printed and bound in Great Britain by
Omnia Books Limited, Glasgow

The Challenge of
CELL CHURCH

Getting to grips with
● cell church values

PHIL POTTER

To my family—at home, at St Marks, and at all points
between Paris and Mwanza, San Diego and Singapore

Acknowledgments

An authentic cell church values the involvement of many at the broadest
level, and the writing of this book has illustrated that. I'm grateful to
many people—family, friends, staff, leaders, church members and
publishers, for all their comments, encouragement and strong support.

In particular, Mo Greenall, my Admin Assistant, has been amazing in
patiently deciphering, typing, collating and chasing. She has worked
with me for nearly twelve years and is an expert with the towel! (See
Chapter 5.)

I've always said that the best kind of cell book would be a cartoon
book written by Ron Bailey. His humour has delighted not only
our own church members but hundreds of others at Christian
conferences, and I'm very grateful for his contribution here.

I'd like to thank everyone at St Mark's for their encouragement, and
a gracious and growing willingness to 'step out of the boat' in faith. In
particular, I'm grateful to Phil Pawley and other leaders in general for
some helpful and constructive remarks along the way. I was also
humbled and touched by the response to my request for written
testimonies for use in the last chapter. The ones included here are only
a sample, but I value the enthusiasm of all those who put pen to paper.

Finally I'm grateful to those who have inspired and introduced me to
cell. In particular, YWAM have put on a string of helpful intro-ductory
conferences, and I recommend them all. I also want to pay tribute to
Howard Astin, an Anglican clergyman who began shouting about cell
church before the rest of us caught on, and also to my brother-in-law,
Tim Butlin, who pestered me into attending my very first cell church
conference! Since then, I've travelled further afield to learn more at
first hand, and have been particularly inspired by the cell church in
Singapore and Hong Kong. Derek Hong and Neville Chamberlain were,
and continue to be, an inspiration in my journey to cell.

Foreword

Phil Potter writes as he speaks—with energy, enthusiasm and conviction. Here is a book about cell churches that is fresh, direct and full of examples and personal illustrations. When people write about their churches there can often be a gap between the image and the reality, but I have seen with my own eyes the substance of what Phil Potter has described here. The teaching that you will find on these pages is both proven and practical. St Mark's Haydock is a vibrant Christian community that serves the local neighbourhood and has experienced remarkable growth.

Phil Potter is sought out by others to share his experiences. He is widely read and widely travelled. I welcome this book for it gives others the opportunity to reflect upon their own churches by comparing them with the story of St Mark's Haydock. Not that Phil Potter wants to see clones of St Mark's around the country, but so that others might apply the principles here to their own unique situations.

I learned much from reading this book and am both encouraged and inspired by the way the people here have responded to the claim of Jesus Christ upon their lives.

The Rt Revd James Jones, Bishop of Liverpool

Recommendations

I warmly recommend *The Challenge of Cell Church*. The challenge of mission today requires a fresh injection of imagination about the shape and culture of the church. If we are to be missionaries in a world where religion is a leisure option, cell church is one of the most helpful and adaptable resources for the task. There are very few people in the Church of England who know more about cell church than Phil Potter. I wholeheartedly commend his work.

The Rt Revd Graham Cray, Bishop of Maidstone

Sometimes when I read cell church material, I find myself thinking, 'Good theory, but what about the practice?' Not so with this book. Phil has a thorough grasp of the subject and only teaches what he has put into practice. This is the best book on cell church I have read.

The Revd Mike Breen, St Thomas Crookes, Sheffield

Contents

Introduction

It may have been the coffee, the weather or the shape of the seats. It could have been the bed of the night before or the busyness of the previous day, but I have to say that the first 24 hours of my first Cell Conference left me completely baffled! It's probably unfair, but when it all became clear on the second morning my reaction was, 'Why didn't you say so in the first place!' Having looked at graphs and tables and listened to some brand new 'jargon', I was in no mood for receiving fresh vision. So I have a lot of sympathy with people whose eyes glaze over and who instantly get bored at the mention of 'Cell Church'. That's partly why I wanted to write something that was simple to read and as easy to grasp as ABC. But why did I want to go and write a whole book about it?

I may be biting off more than I can chew here, but this is a book I want to see in people's hands because I believe it's a vision that can change hearts. How many times have you dreamed of a church that grows and multiplies? How many times have you longed for God to transform your small group? How many times have you wanted to see a good sermon worked out and applied in the life of the church? How many times have you wished that Christians could be real with each other—more loving, more available, adaptable and accountable? How many times have you asked God to move in your ministry without the need for some pastoral professional alongside? And how many friends would you want to be touched and drawn into the Christian faith without being embarrassed about the process? All those questions and more, I believe, are answered in the vision for cell church.

Not everything 'cell' offers is new—far from it. I remember when the Alpha course was first introduced and how many of us felt that it contained little that was new. Much of the teaching we'd been trying to impart for years, often in small groups. But the genius and beauty of Alpha is that it gathers the very best practices and the very best values from all the other courses and puts them together in a fresher and more relevant way. Not only that, but it takes out the 'cringe factors' and puts in a few 'cutting edge' features, emphasizing things like process, presentation and the need for spiritual power. The results, of course, have been phenomenal, not least in enabling the smallest, weakest church to do evangelism in practical and effective ways. As you can see, I'm enthusiastic about Alpha! And I'm passionate about 'Cell' for the very same reasons. All the values I've ever tried to teach, and all the vision I've been striving to build, are to be found in the cell church movement, but they've been put together in a way that can really work for any church and at every level.

Having made the claim, I'll now try and make the case, but first let me go back to that conference. The second 24 hours were exhilarating as the speakers hit the target again and again on every point of need and piece of baggage I'd happened to bring along. How could the church grow? How could every member feel a part? How could they all be mobilized for mission? How could we start looking out instead of in? This time, however, it wasn't just a strategy tagged on, but a whole set of values to be reaffirmed and a whole new vision to be released. I may not remember the graphs and tables, but I do recall some very quotable quotes that summed up the essence of 'cell'. I'll refer to these in appropriate places, but for now let me recall the story that left me saying, 'Yes Lord, I'll go for it!' It went something like this:

In the 1960s, Swiss watch makers apparently still controlled 88 per cent of the market with beautifully crafted timepieces. Around that time, a thing called 'quartz' was invented. It fascinated the Swiss and really impressed them. They constructed a watch using the new invention, but at the end of the day they decided, 'It isn't really a watch as we know watches.' They showed it to other companies, exhibiting and illuminating it in glass cases, but didn't bother with the patent. One day, a couple of Japanese businessmen arrived and loved what they saw. They went away and started producing electronic quartz watches. Everybody today wears quartz watches and yet the Swiss have less than 10 per cent of the market and less than 20 per cent of the profit!

That little story didn't just amuse me—it challenged me profoundly to act on the message it sends. In fact I agree with those who say that our traditional home groups have reached their 'sell by' date. I also believe that this little word 'cell' is going to be on every church member's lips by the end of the decade. People like Bill Beckham and Ralph Neighbour have (through the American market) provided us with some excellent teaching on the subject in conferences and books, and I'm very grateful to them. I offer this shorter addition with three simple aims:

- to explain it to the uninitiated;
- to sell it to the unconverted;
- to offer it as a resource to those who want to implement it.

With these aims in mind, I've tried first of all to take away some of the jargon that's connected with the subject—apart, of course, from the word 'cell'. It may be helpful at the beginning to differentiate between the phrase 'cell group' and 'cell church'. 'Cell church' (or cell-based church) refers to a collective total of groups that make up a distinct Christian community, as opposed to the words 'cell' and 'cell group' which refer to one single small group.

As the writing of the book progressed, I decided to provide a cell outline at the end of each chapter. I hope these may be helpful for home groups and leadership teams considering cell church, or those who are in the early stages of transition. Not only do they give the flavour of a typical cell group programme, but I hope they will help the whole process of thinking it through and sharpening vision.

And finally, for those who are sick of all the words, just enjoy the cartoons at the end. For me, they say it all!

Chapter 1

Doing Time

OK, so the word 'cell' makes you think about Strangeways and Wormwood Scrubs! And what was wrong with the phrase 'home groups' (or 'house groups') in the first place? Isn't this just another tacky import of jargon and window dressing to add to what we've already got? What's the difference between a house group and a cell group, anyway?

All good questions, and to be really honest, if you run a house group the way it was meant to be run, then there may be very little difference at all at first sight. If we're honest, though, many of us have had a love-hate relationship with house groups for some time now, and in most churches they tend to have had a pretty chequered history, with peaks and troughs of popularity, often depending on how much time there actually is in the church calendar to get on and do them.

Before we considered cell, our own church had seen a steady dwindling from 25 groups to 15, largely because our programme was overbusy, good leaders overworked and a review was well overdue. My first Cell Conference gave me the opportunity to begin this, but it gave a whole lot more besides. It didn't take long to re-establish the fundamental importance of small groups, but what it gave me in addition was a wake-up call to their pivotal importance. More than that, it offered a strategy to put them at the very heart of the church's life where they really could have the number one call on people's commitment that they deserved.

Number one commitment? Doesn't that mean that small group life is actually as important, if not more so, than Sunday services? Well, I have to come clean at the very beginning and say yes. To have a single cell is to have an authentic church. Having said that, however, let me also say that only one month after moving into a cell church model, the number of weekly communicants at our Sunday services had risen by 50! By the end of our first year, our main service had multiplied into three separate services—two in the morning and one in the afternoon.

Now I can't say that was all due to an instant impact on the unchurched community (I wish!), but what I can say is that the shift in focus from Sunday to cell had a profound and lasting effect on the congregation itself. People on the fringe were suddenly appearing more regularly. People who'd been missing had come back. People who'd been hit-and-miss in attendance were becoming more consistent and 'once a month-ers' were now coming once a week. In other words, as the whole life of the church was being refocused around its cell life, the congregational life was being renewed and refreshed and strengthened. Instead of Sundays being the main source of inspiration and recuperation for the week ahead, they were now becoming the major time of celebration where cells could gather for praise and worship and even greater doses of what they'd already been receiving during the week. People were rediscovering that the church is a seven-day-a-week shared experience and not just a spectator Sunday sport!

So, what was different? What had changed inside the groups that now inspired 350 people to attend where only 150 had previously? And what made it begin to impact the life of the church? What made it suddenly feel right where previously we'd obviously got it wrong? And what had been killing off the groups in the first place?

Let's talk about that before we go much further, because we need to see where small groups often do go wrong. The truth is that most groups are very strong in some areas and weak in others, depending on the make-up and history of the group itself. But then I expect most of us have had a few negative experiences in groups, and maybe some of us have even felt as if we're trapped in prison doing time! The first step, then, is to recognize the weaknesses that are there and to ask how we can work consistently at all the potential strengths. Here are half a dozen small group killers that you may well recognize and groan at:

1. The Club: strong on membership, weak on community

The feeling here is that house group is just something we do on a Wednesday night at 8.00pm. It's something we love doing and we're proud to be members, but during the six days in between we rarely talk to each other and never really care what's going on in the other members' lives. In other words, we treat it on the same level as going to the pub or attending any local club. It's definitely a membership thing but in terms of commitment it barely begins to register on the friends-and-relationships scale. That's not to say that everyone isn't very friendly and helpful at the meeting. But if a pastoral issue or practical problem arises, then this group may not even be aware of it, or will automatically assume that the vicar or the care team or whoever will deal with it first.

2. The Class: strong on study, weak on ministry

This is a group where Bible study is the dominant task, and great effort goes into both preparation and discussion. The danger comes when the concern for truth about God and Bible knowledge becomes a smokescreen for avoiding the need for self-knowledge. It's the kind of group where we hide behind our Bibles and cherish important words like 'maturity' and 'depth', and the more study we do and the more commentaries and concordances we use, the better the group.

But what's the point of asking what the Bible means, if we don't then ask the question, 'How does this apply to me in my situation, and what is God saying to me?' And when he does start speaking and I start applying his word, then the one thing I really need is ministry. I want someone to encourage me and identify with the issues, and then pray with me in a helpful and practical way. When Bible study is really effective, the whole group should come to that same position and if time isn't allowed for that, then how much truth and what kind of learning have we really taken on board?

3. The Clinic: strong on caring, weak on discipline

This group is everyone's dream when we're looking for sympathy or are genuinely in need of care. Where there is a problem, quality time will be given to listening and loving people through it. Again, it's a group with a great deal to offer but it can also be fraught with danger. Taken to extremes, the caring group degenerates quickly into a very large dustbin where all my worries, hurts and hassles can be unloaded, and by the time the whole group's done that, then, boy, are we depressed! What's more, there's a very real danger here of sticking plasters on deeper wounds that are going to keep on festering without proper attention.

The clinic is a group that's in danger of trying to make people happy instead of making them whole. When we encourage each other, we don't just sympathize and affirm that being a Christian's a struggle, we try and turn the 'why' questions into 'what': what is God trying to say to me and what does he want to do? The clinic's main concern is happiness: how can I make the hurting happy again? But if we really care for each other, what we want above all is to make each other like Christ. That, in the end, is what makes us really happy, and simply applying a plaster is not always the best answer. It also turns the group into a dumping ground for unresolved rubbish.

4. The Clan: strong on unity, weak on vulnerability

A group that's become a clan has a very strong identity, and that usually means they have a bee in their bonnet about something! They might be very strong on the power of prayer, or the importance of mission, or 'standing on the word', and they'll pursue that common interest with a passion. Whenever they meet, all their time and energy will go into defending and developing the thing that they're really hot on, so much so that they never actually get around to taking off their armour and becoming vulnerable to each other. The point here is that it's all very well being strong on unity and identity, but it's a total waste of time if we never identify our weaknesses and unite around our frailty. The clan presents such a strong corporate face that no one has a chance to show a personal face and share their real selves.

5. The Closet: strong on protection, weak on nurturing gifts

I suppose you could call this group the holy huddle. It's a group that concentrates on keeping things the way they are. And why? Because the group is very nice as it is, thank you very much, and we don't want to rock the boat or put people off or wind anyone up. If the leader wants to give us a little sermon each week, that's fine—it's his group. If somebody has always offered their home and hospitality, it's not very wise to suggest alternative venues. If two or three members gently disrupt the group and inhibit others, it may not be helpful to challenge them.

Unfortunately, a group like this becomes so claustrophobic that people can't breathe and they certainly can't grow. There may be people in that group who are potential leaders, and others who are capable of exercising all kinds of gifts, if we'll only let them. This group needs to get out of the closet, knock down a few restricting walls and then get producing. It needs to draw out the potential, release the talent and nurture the hidden gifts.

6. The Clique: strong on belonging, weak on reproducing

I think this is often the biggest danger for 'successful' groups. We become so effective in learning and sharing together and generally meeting each other's needs that we secretly want to bottle up the formula and preserve what we've got. At last we've found a place where we belong and people we can relate to. So why go and spoil it all by bringing in new people? Often, we can find quite plausible excuses like the size of our home or the make-up of the group or the stage that we're at, but in the end there's a strong instinct in us all that says, 'I'd rather belong than reproduce.'

This is where cell groups become fundamentally different from traditional groups, because in time they increasingly focus outwards till the whole group is enabled and equipped to be effective witnesses and evangelists. That means a little group of six is eventually going to grow beyond twelve people and actually give birth to a brand new group as a result. And when it does, there's a whole ethos in place that enables people to let it happen. Instead of mourning the death of a group, cell members learn to celebrate a birth! In the cell church, belonging feels good, but reproducing feels right.

The 'cell' word

Speaking about 'feeling right', when I first investigated cell church, I was immediately drawn by the potential of weeding out all those weaknesses and drawing out all the strengths. As far as I could see, the cell church had a very strong agenda and strategy for producing community, ministry, discipling, vulnerability, nurturing gifts and multiplying members, and that excited me. Since then I've come to appreciate the word 'cell' in a whole new way. I'm not a scientist, but I do understand that our bodies are made up of millions of living cells, each and every one involved in keeping the body alive and active. Expanding, then, on that wonderful picture of the body of Christ that we talk about so often, what do we need to take on board when we think about the cells that make up the human body?

1. They are living and life-giving

Someone describing the world of cells as they appear under a microscope wrote this: 'A universe sprang to life. Hundreds of organisms crowded into view: delicate, single-celled globes of crystal, breathing, whirling, flitting sideways, excited by the warmth of my microscope light…'.[1] Cells are not just a bunch of chemicals that get switched on and off to fulfil a function. They have life and power and purpose. And when a small group starts doing all that it's capable of doing, it becomes far more than a meeting. A house group meets, but a cell becomes a whole way of life, a community that's growing and serving and constantly in touch with its members.

2. They are small and efficient

Cells are one of the smallest units of life, and although they vary in size, they are microscopically small. To be seen, they must be magnified many times and our bodies are made up of billions of them. And yet it's inside the cell that energy is actually made available for the whole body to function. Despite their size, cells are tiny little power houses! In the same way, a small cell group is the perfect environment for seeing God's power released. A basic principle in the cell church is that 'small is beautiful'. One of its greatest strengths is in recognizing that when groups are too large, people get lost, ignored and left out, and the agendas become too large as well. The result is often to stifle its purpose, sap its energy and drain away its life.

When St Mark's had only three house groups, one was actually called 'the main group' for a while because that particular gathering could easily top 30 people on a good day. Not surprisingly, the groups were not growing and involvement remained static. A cell group, however, can often begin with as few as six people. Over time it aims to develop and empower those people from being passive members, who are often doing very little in the church, into active ministers with a very real role and a desire to serve.

3. They co-operate and serve

Two things about biological cells are particularly remarkable. Although chemically they are very alike, visually and functionally they can be as different as animals in a zoo. And yet they move and work together in incredible harmony. And even more amazing is the way they deliberately let go of all but one or two abilities in order to specialize in a single task. Apparently cells are experts at taking turns and dividing up labour!

Now cell group members may take a lot longer to learn the art, but each and every person is encouraged to get involved in a servant way, discovering where they can fit in and what they can offer in gifts and skills and time. Like the human body, there's a carefully ordered structure to ensure that no one takes on too much, and nobody gets left to one side. Mind you, there's another analogy here because occasionally a cell can choose to live inside the body and share its benefits while keeping itself totally independent. Those cells become parasites and are called cancers!

4. They need each other to function properly

There are millions of cells inside a hand alone, but a hand can quickly be rendered useless by the breakdown of a handful of tiny nerve cells, for example, when somebody has Hansen's disease (leprosy). Just the breakdown of one type of cell can cause havoc with the whole organ. Every active cell communicates and co-operates constantly with the rest of the body; and in the cell church, although at one level every cell group can operate as a fully functioning church, there's still a major emphasis on unity of purpose and vision, on working together and communicating at every turn. In every cell church, there's a carefully laid-out network of mutual support and shared leadership to enable the whole body to move and grow together. And unlike the human body, when one of the cells breaks down it can soon be rebuilt with the help of other cells.

5. They share the same ingredients

Although there's a vast variety of different cells that make up the body, they do still share a single ingredient that guarantees a single overall goal. It's called DNA and all the cells in one body contain it, sending out the same basic blueprint of instructions to each and every cell. At the end of the day, a cell church is far more than a clever structure with a clear religious purpose. It's a living thing that's been infused with the DNA of Jesus—'Christ in you, the hope of glory' (Colossians 1:27). Everything a cell aims to do is centred on him and his teaching, and that's what makes it authentically 'church'. In fact, that is what attracted me to embrace the whole package, because it increasingly appears to be the best possible vehicle in our time for enabling people to follow Jesus.

6. They grow and multiply

One of the unique features of white blood cells in the body is that they don't have a very long life in themselves, because they go on multiplying. Similarly, the cell group is uniquely different because its chief and ultimate aim is to grow and then multiply. It literally lives to divide and if it doesn't, it eventually degenerates and loses its life. I don't really know of one home group that hasn't eventually dried up and died when it's failed to grow. Sometimes a group can seem to thrive for year after year but eventually, even if it's through sheer old age, the group passes its sell-by date and loses its reason for existence.

On the other hand, let's just reflect for a moment on some of the more dramatic examples of cell church multiplication.

Perhaps the most famous example is Dr Paul Yonggi Cho's story of his church in Seoul, South Korea.[2] He began his ministry in the 1950s with five people, and within ten years his church had grown to two thousand. At this size, however, he found it increasingly difficult to pastor along traditional lines. He said, 'I was only 28 years old, but my body was a wreck.' Let's face it, many of our leaders end up feeling like this. Ministry is a tiring and tough job and we need all the help we can get. Yonggi Cho found it through focusing on a cell-based model, and today his church is fast approaching a million members.

Other exciting examples are well documented in Howard Astin's Book, *Body and Cell*,[3] as well as Ralph Neighbour's *Where Do We Go From Here?*[4] What I think is particularly exciting, however, is a growing transformation of smaller churches. It isn't just the super-leaders who are seeing the fruit of the cell church approach. In Hong Kong, for example, all the churches recently did a survey of their shift in membership over the past five years. They discovered that, as the population grew by nearly 13 per cent, the church as a whole in that period actually shrank by 23 per cent. There are now 118 churches in Hong Kong (of all denominations) that have become cell churches or are in the process of doing so (that's about 20 per cent of the total). Those churches were so horrified by the results of the survey that together they decided to conduct their own. They discovered that in the same period, their cell churches had grown by 130 per cent (in other words, ten times the population growth), and the vast majority of their new members were all new Christians. Meanwhile, a few sums to work out the true figure of decline in most of the other Hong Kong churches leaves a very sad picture.

I'd hate this chapter to give the impression that cell church is all about success and number chasing. I hope I've given the impression that rather it is about coveting quality and authenticity, but you can check that out in the chapters ahead. Nor would I want to pretend that cell church provides an easy, painless formula for being church.

There's no such thing, and this is a vision like any other, where that which costs nothing is worth nothing.

When I think of prison cells I often think of the Church in China, where there are so many examples of persecution. One pastor spoke at a national leaders' conference here a few years ago. He spoke of his twenty years in solitary confinement, put to work each day in a pool of human waste. He also spoke of his faith and his walk with God and said that even in that prison 'the cesspool became my private garden' for worship and praise. Meanwhile, the Church in his land has seen the most rapid church growth in the history of Christianity, despite the persecution. Never before, anywhere in the world, have so many accepted Christ in such a short period of time. Indeed, when the borders of China were opened again after the Cultural Revolution, Christians in the West expected to find a dying and desecrated Church. The buildings may have disappeared, but they soon discovered that a miracle had taken place, one that continues today.

How does the Church survive in these places and why does it thrive through the fires of persecution? Apart from the amazing testimonies of people like the Chinese pastor, that speak of an awesome and gracious move of God in the face of suffering, I can't help thinking that when the outward facade of the Church is stripped away completely, what's so often left in these places is huge numbers of tiny cells, worshipping, learning, ministering together, and actually growing!

Let me close the chapter with the words of Samuel Rutherford, the 17th-century pastor and theologian who was imprisoned and persecuted for his faith. When he found himself in prison, he wrote this in his diary: 'Jesus Christ came into my cell last night, and every stone flashed like a ruby!' I would never pretend that cell groups don't occasionally feel like prison. They can, as we'll see, be frustrating, challenging and even painful, but they also reverberate with the life and joy of our faith. And anyway, what's our faith about if it doesn't involve a little counting the cost and 'doing time' for the kingdom?

Cell outline

These outlines are particularly geared to help your group discuss the contents of each chapter and consider the challenge of cells. The Word sections are therefore not heavily based on particular Bible passages. They should be used selectively, so that you don't run out of time for the Witness section. A typical cell meeting might aim to spend fifteen minutes on the Welcome, fifteen minutes in Worship, an hour on the Word, and half an hour on the Witness. Please read the explanation of the four Ws in Chapter 2 before using the first outline. Remember that the Welcome and Worship sections in particular are only suggestions. If you don't feel comfortable using these particular ideas, be creative, but follow the principles!

Finally, I realize that for churches considering cell for the first time, it may be very difficult to cover all the issues raised in a single chapter at one meeting. It may be appropriate to spend a couple of meetings discussing the content of one or two of the chapters, particularly in Chapter 8. Again, be flexible, but try to have a true taste of a typical cell programme.

Welcome

If you were locked up in a prison cell and allowed to keep hold of one personal item what would it be (apart from your Bible!)?

Worship

- Build this time around the theme of freedom to worship!
- Play a reflective piece of music. Think about all you would miss if you were locked away for your faith, and reflect on the freedom you have to meet with others in fellowship.
- Use Paul's letter to the Philippians as a tool to help you. Glancing through chapter 1, meditate on the verses that stand out as you

read them, mindful that they are written from prison. Read out any that you feel would be particularly helpful to the group.

- After a few minutes of personal reflection, move into a time for corporate prayer. Express the things you are thankful for, with simple one-line prayers; for example, 'Thank you, Lord, for the freedom we had to come here today.'
- End this section by reading Philippians 2:1–4. Invite someone to close in prayer, asking God to help you be mindful of each other's needs and interests as you talk together about the life of your group.

Word

'The truth is that most groups are very strong in some areas and weak in others.'

1. Discuss the list of six cell killers:
   - The Club
   - The Class
   - The Clinic
   - The Clan
   - The Closet
   - The Clique

Applying this list to your own group, allow each person to highlight one area of strength and one area of weakness. Is there a common thread of opinion about the health of the group?

2. Reflect together on the image of cells in the body:
   - They are living and life-giving
   - They are small and efficient
   - They co-operate and serve
   - They need each other to function properly
   - They share the same ingredients
   - They grow and multiply

Which of these do you find most attractive and would like to see developing further inside your group?

Witness

Summarize what you have shared by identifying the areas for which you feel most thankful and the areas in which you feel most challenged.

Pray together for the development of your group and ask God to help you:

- nurture the strengths
- address the weaknesses

Chapter 2

Getting into Shape

Cellulite. There's another good 'cell' word! I only know three things about cellulite. One is that it's trapped fat that you neither need nor want. The second is that women's magazines talk a lot about how you can get rid of it. And the third thing is that men don't get it (he says smugly)! There's an hilarious character in a recent Libby Purves novel, *More Lives Than One*, who runs a very popular keep-fit class called 'Positively Plump'. The motto of the class is 'Nothing wrong with fat as long as you keep it moving'! Now when you think about it, there's a good illustration here because the body of Christ is certainly no supermodel. We're never going to find the perfect figure of a church this side of heaven, and many of our churches at times look decidedly unexercised, ill-proportioned and overweight. But then, hey, there's nothing wrong with fat as long as you keep it moving!

Jesus was never interested in having a bride that's an outward beauty freak (Revelation 19:7–8). He's far more interested in the inner beauty of righteousness (v. 7) and the importance of a healthy body, and a healthy body keeps moving. It stays in shape by keeping active and watching its diet, concentrating on doing and absorbing the things that are good for it. Continuing with this picture, then, the cell church model is like a diet and exercise plan. It's a way of helping the Church to stay in shape and live healthily and, above all, to keep moving. In this chapter, I want to spell out the plan in practical terms, drawing out the key factors that make a cell church uniquely different from traditional church.

Choosing the right plan

Look along the shelves of any health-and-diet section and you'll find an amazing array of books. Some say that it's all about what you eat and others emphasize what you shouldn't eat. Some of them focus on diet and others on exercise, and all of them claim that their way is best! Seeing the choice and the differing claims can make you cynical, and seeing the word 'cell' can make you wonder if this is just another religious fad. But then one or two of the books present you with an overview. They spell out the key principles and emphasize what's important in all the different approaches, leaving you to decide what is most helpful for you. Now at first sight the cell church model may seem a little too prescriptive and a bit like an over-zealous health book, but as you look at it more closely it does two things. First, it establishes values and principles that are non-negotiable. All of these are biblical values and shouldn't give Christians any great problem. It then provides a very clear structure in which those values can be worked out, and within that structure gives enormous flexibility for God to encourage his church at different stages and in different cultures.

So where does the plan begin? Well, as the phrase 'cell church' suggests, the focus on small group life is paramount. In the Gospels we find Jesus relating in depth to a very small group. He may have chosen many ways to introduce and model kingdom values but the way he went about choosing the apostles is striking. Luke tells us (in chapter 6) that Jesus spent the whole night in prayer before he called the Twelve. He also tells us that 'a large crowd of his disciples' was waiting in anticipation there, as well as 'a great number' of other interested people (v. 17). What I find myself wondering is how on earth all the other disciples felt when Jesus reappeared and said, 'I'm just going to concentrate on twelve! I love you all, but I'm going to share my life much more deeply with these twelve for now.' If you and I had been there, we may have looked at his choices and questioned whether we still wanted to follow him. Why those particular men? And why the specialization? Why the quality time for the few? Why don't we all just live and move around together in a single giant community?

By the time the early Church became established it was indeed a powerful community, but all the evidence suggests that the small group remained the basic and essential unit of the Church's life for the first two centuries. We know, for instance, that there were no church buildings. Certainly we see continuing use of the temple for a while for prayer, preaching and teaching (Acts 2:46). But as we read through the New Testament the evidence mounts of a church that met inside homes in small groups. In Acts there are various accounts of homes being used for prayer (Acts 12:12); breaking of bread (Acts 2:46; 20:7); evenings of fellowship (Acts 21:7); evangelistic meetings (Acts 5:42; 10:22; 16:32); and one-to-one nurture gatherings (Acts 18:26). Later on, Paul sent greetings to churches in the homes of Priscilla and Aquila (Romans 16:5), Nympha (Colossians 4:15) and Philemon (Philemon 1:2).

Long before that, Moses had been shown the need for ministry to the smaller group. Following Jethro's advice he appointed 60,000 leaders of tens as the problems, burdens and disputes increased (Exodus 18:13–26). Virtually every movement of spiritual renewal in the Christian Church has been accompanied by a return to the small group. One of the more famous examples is John Wesley's movement, and we'll return to that later. Another glance into Church history reveals names like Francis of Assisi, who gathered his disciples together in small groups for training, sharing, study and prayer. It also reveals other movements such as the early Lutherans, the Pietists, and the Holiness movement that swept America in the late 1800s and led towards modern Pentecostalism. Small has been beautiful for a very long time in the story of God's people, and that's what the cell church model emphasizes above all else in affirming what it is to be church.

But what does that mean in practical terms? It means, first of all, that anyone considering cell church must be willing to work out the principle that cell is central. It means that over a period of time there's going to be a subtle but radical shift in the life of a congregation. Eventually the whole fellowship is going to understand that the cell group has become the major focus in that church's life. No longer will they define membership in terms of how many are turning out to services on a Sunday, but rather how many are involved in cells. That doesn't mean, of course, that those who aren't involved in cells are now excluded from membership. But ultimately—possibly only after a few years—there'll be a new generation of Christians who see the cell as the primary outward expression of belonging to the body of Christ. And yet, as I mentioned earlier, main services will continue to thrive, a major rallying point for all the cells to come and celebrate their faith together. How can that work? Very simply, the more people come to cell and learn the value of fellowship, worship and commitment, the more they come to understand the value of Sunday itself.

Now all that may be quite a leap for traditional congregations but increasingly it appears to meet the needs and expectations of new members. We've found in our own church, for instance, that although the Alpha course has provided the perfect entry to the faith for many enquirers, the jump into Sunday worship has been too great when they've reached the end of the course. They've come to value the small group and the growing network of relationships, but the Sunday service with all its unspoken rules and rituals is just too much for the typical unchurched seeker (and I like to feel that our church is pretty free and easy!). What we've found is that more and more people are coming to faith with a passionate commitment to the cell, but it takes anything from a couple of months to a couple of years for a new believer to make the transition into the larger church community and embrace some of its other established traditions, like liturgy, ceremony and ritual.

Thinking about this balance between services and cell, Bill Beckham has offered a helpful picture in his image of 'the two-winged church'.[5] He compares the church to a bird with two wings—a reflection of the two sides of its creator's own nature: his transcendent greatness on the one hand, and his immanent and intimate closeness on the other. He talks about one of the church's wings being large-group celebration and the other wing small-group community, and a bird, of course, needs both wings to fly. When one of the wings is weakened, the bird finds it very difficult to get off the ground, and when it does it will tend to lose its sense of direction and fly around in circles. Both wings are important, and so a cell church will have no desire to lose its own sense of direction by shunning the larger expression of community. Equally, a congregation will feel the loss if it doesn't embrace the smaller expression of God's immanent love. How many have drifted away from Sunday worship because they 'felt lost in the crowd'?

Getting back to the diet, however, there has to be a plan and the plan here begins with a determination to put cells at the centre of church life.

Cutting out and cutting down

Now comes the painful bit! Invariably diet and exercise plans require a disciplined regime and the cell church is no different. If you want to get into shape, some things have to go while new habits are introduced, and in the cell church, pruning is essential. It's no good agreeing that small group life is fundamental and essential, only to find that there isn't room in our lives to do it! This was our problem in Haydock. The people who went missing from our house groups were ironically but increasingly our most committed. As more and more interesting programmes and ministries were introduced into the church, more and more members (and especially our leaders) began to get bogged down. As they became more involved in their ministries, they became less involved in relationships and even less inclined to belong to any home group. Eventually, many members had several responsibilities within the church and were showing signs of spiritual dryness and faith decay. Sunday was becoming the sole place for feeding and refreshment, and many of them were too involved in service duties even to benefit there. In short, what was needed in their lives and the church's life was some heavy pruning.

We began the process by pruning our diaries. We took on board that cell is central and agreed that all of us would make it our first priority. Leaders and members who had left their small group agreed to be part of a cell group. We quickly discovered that leaders had often been doing two or three jobs in the church and that one or two would definitely have to go. That in itself felt quite hairy because potentially there were going to be no leaders and lots of jobs! Amazingly, however, we found that as spaces were created, the jobs were filled with newer people we'd never even thought of. At the same time we found that people came into cells, discovered their gifts and began serving. Already it was beginning to feel like tending a fertile garden. Heavy pruning looks a little ruthless at first, but then the new buds appear and the growth takes off again with a vengeance. Before long, you're sitting in the garden enjoying the fruit.

The second thing we had to prune was our programmes. Like many churches, we had a tendency to add on new ministries instead of replacing them. When we looked at the church diary there was no way we could promote cell and encourage people's involvement without significantly thinning what was already there. But it didn't take long to see that what was already there needed examining anyway. I'd often reminded the church of David Watson's thoughts when he wrote:

At least once a year, ruthless questions need to be asked in an attitude of prayer and submission to God about the whole pattern of our services, our meetings and organizations and buildings.
- *Are they achieving anything today?*
- *Are they the best use of time and money today?*
- *Are they helping to build up the Body of Christ today?*
- *Are they assisting the church in evangelism today?*
- *Are they God's best plan for today?*

Their value yesterday is not the important point. Christian work is constantly crippled by clinging to blessings and traditions of the past. God is not the God of yesterday. He is the God of today... Heaven forbid that we should continue playing religious games in one corner when the cloud and fire of God's presence have moved to another.[6]

Making changes can be painful and yet so liberating. As we began looking for the 'cloud and fire' in our own programmes, it became obvious what we had to do and where we needed to do it. For instance, the playgroup leaders said, 'We haven't got time for cell. The playgroup meets every single day and we haven't got anything left to give'. In fact that was obvious. They were tired and discouraged and dry and they badly needed a place of refreshment. They also needed a place where they could receive fresh vision for their ministry and witness. We agreed then, to cancel a whole session of playgroup so that the team could meet as a cell on that afternoon. Not only were we offering them a break and some refreshment, but also some quality time to pray and plan around their ministry, not least in reaching out to all those young parents they were regularly meeting. We began to see that, in time, this would lead to a transformation of both the hearts of the leaders and their vision for the ministry.

On another front, we used to have a men's fellowship with speakers, sports and breakfasts, and a team to run the events and look after our men. Applying the principle, we agreed that everything the team organized should directly serve and benefit the cells, and eventually be done by the cells. The group has now been replaced with a men's cell which organizes strategic events as part of their own witness.

Dietary cut-downs can irritate at first, but we soon enjoy the benefits and get used to the new habits. Cutting out and cutting down has certainly made St Mark's feel leaner, fitter and a whole lot happier. Even the cell meetings themselves keep to a two-hour programme. We ask people not to increase this so that members can feel that the cell meeting is not a huge commitment. Of course, people are free to stay on after the programme is finished, but they also need to feel that this is a commitment that can be fitted into the busiest of schedules. Indeed, some of our busiest people may decide not to meet during the conventional evening or daytime slot, but over a meal or early in the evening, or whenever. Putting a time limit on the progamme itself enables people to think and plan more flexibly before making the commitment to come. It also takes seriously the fact that we now live in a frenetic and complex world where 'cutting out and cutting down' is a vital part of 'getting a life'! But now we come to the diet itself!

Sticking to the diet

This is referred to by one leader as 'mother's meal', meaning mother knows best when it comes to nutrition—too many chips and too little veg is bad for the child! The cell programme itself follows a carefully laid-out pattern, a simple four-point plan that offers the basic nutrition that every cell group needs. Whenever the cell meets the four points are covered. These are known as the four Ws—Welcome, Worship, Word and Witness (or Works). Such a plan may seem a little stifling and prescriptive, but let me give you two good reasons for following it. First of all, it puts less pressure on the cell leader in planning and steering the group. Instead of always thinking, 'What shall we do this week and how will I do it?' the leader has a ready-made plan that is very simple to apply. To the few who might object that it stifles creativity and insults their intelligence, the programme still has a great deal of flexibility.

Often, however, the greater concern by far is how on earth we are going to find and train the number of cell leaders needed. Many people have never led a group before and we feel we can't possibly throw them in at the deep end. This is precisely the kind of problem we faced at St Mark's. Not many of us come from a professional background and few have had experience in leading small groups. But again and again we've found that the four Ws have been an invaluable tool in building confidence and easing the load, guiding the leader through each and every meeting step by step.

The second benefit of structure is that it acts as a checklist in guarding against the small group killers we described in the previous chapter. When you think about it, every worship service has a form of liturgy and a structure that it follows. Even where it may not be as obvious as an Anglican or Roman Catholic liturgy, the most relaxed services have a very clear agenda. Usually they will include an element of praise, of confession and intercession, and then a session that focuses on the word of God, often followed by a form of response, whether it be prayer ministry or a simple sending-out with a blessing. As leaders, we follow these patterns automatically and we find them helpful in keeping our balance. In the same way, the four Ws offer a progressive pattern, a kind of healthy eating menu that begins with an appetiser and ends with dessert.

Welcome

In the Welcome section, there's a special emphasis on gathering and helping the whole group gel together. Instead of allowing time to slide and eventually stumbling into the programme, this section gives a focused start and a sense of direction to the meeting. It usually begins with an icebreaker, a question with a light-hearted edge. Here are a few examples:

- If you could spend the rest of your life doing exactly what you wanted, what would you do?
- If you were shipwrecked on a desert island, what one item would you want to have with you?
- If you could spend the day with a Bible character, who would it be and why?
- What is your favourite time of day and why?
- What are three of your favourite activities?
- If you could ask God one question now (with a guaranteed answer) what would it be?

At St Mark's we often go one step further and try to link the icebreaker with the overall theme of the session. For example:

- On the theme of patience: What makes you most impatient and why?
- On the theme of thankfulness: Name one thing you've felt thankful for over the past week.
- On the theme of the manna the Israelites ate in the desert (even obscure themes lend themselves to the idea): What for you is the most boring meal in the world and why?

Now I have to admit that when I was first introduced to cell church, I had no vision for icebreakers whatsoever, and the four Ws were immediately going to be reduced to three! I thought they were either a gimmick or at best an unhelpful import from an alien culture, and my English reserve cried 'embarrassing'! Since then I've not only come to enjoy and value them, but to see them as absolutely fundamental to the overall programme. Let me give you three good reasons for the use of icebreakers.

One: They provide a common focus by drawing everybody into discussion at the very beginning. Often a group may have a buzz about it as people arrive, but the good vibes may only be coming from a dominant few, while others are left unnoticed on the outside of the conversation. The shy person may be feeling excluded, the new person may be feeling embarrassed, and the hurting person may be feeling alienated. A good icebreaker will enable each and every person to contribute and at the same time convey to others a little of 'where they're at'. The questions will always be easy and interesting and often amusing, but if someone blatantly isn't in the mood, the group is alerted and the leader can address the problem. Sometimes it might simply be a case of bad day blues and the person needs a little space. The need is registered and the group backs off. Other times an icebreaker may break open a little more than is intended, and a major need or hurt is immediately shared. I've known some meetings leap swiftly from icebreaker to prayer ministry and some very moving times have been spent in sharing and ministering to some serious needs. Usually, though, the icebreaker simply gets the group chatting and sharing and paves the way for the rest of the meeting.

Two: They relax people, especially at the end of a busy day when people may have rushed in from a day at work and are feeling weary or stressed. Good icebreakers are completely stress-free because there are no right answers and every answer is important. Having said that, they're as open to abuse and misuse as any other tool, and I heard one cell member refer to them recently as 'icemakers'! Certainly I have to confess to times when I have sat and cringed as a tricky, irrelevant or just plain boring question has been asked and everyone has frozen up.

Indeed, now that we have over 40 cells of every imaginable shade, we've realized that a good icebreaker in one group is going to be an appalling one in another. That's why we give everyone a list of 50 general icebreakers (see Appendix 2) plus a resource list of other ideas from various books. If a suggested icebreaker doesn't fit, people are free to choose something else. Of course, some groups still boast that they don't need one, and sometimes that may well be the case. A cell may gather and they're all breaking the ice happily. The more I observe and lead small groups, however, the more off-weeks I encounter and the more I see the need for as much assistance as the tools can offer!

Three: They unearth a goldmine of interesting, important and practical information about all the people in the group, and I think this is what I love most about icebreakers, because in time they become an invaluable pastoral tool. When we first began our cell programme, the whole church seemed to be reverberating with comments like, 'I never knew that about so-and-so'; 'I feel I'm getting to know people for the very first time'; and 'Now I understand where they're coming from.' And all this is done with a few minutes' fun!

Worship

People have often been disappointed by small-group worship, maybe because they've found it to be a poor imitation of the larger celebration. Their mistake, of course, is in looking for the same experience. They're tempted to think that worship invariably involves live music, but when they discover there are no musicians in the group (or one rather bad one!), they assume that worship will have to go on the back burner. When a cell group meets, however, there are two principles to take on board. The first is that we need an encounter with God, and the second is that we *don't* need a guitar to do it! But notice where the worship appears in the programme. It doesn't appear before the Welcome, because we want people to be relaxed as they enter worship. And it comes before the Word, because we recognize that all the Bible study and discussion in the world will never connect unless we've first connected with the Lord himself.

How do we do it? You can see from the cell notes at the end of each chapter that a range of simple, creative worship ideas has been suggested, based on a theme and a scripture passage. These may concentrate on praise one week, confession or thankfulness on another, or all three together. The level of spontaneous involvement will vary depending on how far the group has developed. One group might have a room full of budding worship leaders, but the assumption is that some of our groups are being gently nurtured into worship from no previous experience. For them, a simple focus with a simple response is all that's required, plus a CD of good worship music in the background!

At the same time worship can also be more activity-based. Sometimes the cell might pass an object around the room (like a scented flower), or place one at the centre (like a lighted candle), then respond in prayer to the message it conveys. Sometimes a photograph or a painting can be used as a focus for praise, and sometimes writing a one-word confession on a piece of paper can become a focus for repentance as it gets torn up and tossed into a common waste-bin. Look out for good ideas from the church's main worship leader, the leadership in general, or from a good book!

The Word

As the name suggests, this section focuses on the word of God, but it is not traditional Bible study. As we've already commented, the danger with a Bible class mentality is that the word of God to me personally may not always emerge. If the emphasis is purely on study and there are no Bible students present, then the group is also in danger of sharing ignorance or simply 'precious thoughts'. So the emphasis in cell groups is on taking established truths and applying them with the question, 'What is God saying to me, or to us as a cell group?' To do this, we often take the main Sunday sermon each week and encourage people to apply its teaching. This is done with just two or three simple and very specific questions that encourage people to share their thoughts and responses and where they may need help. The questions in themselves should be so simple that they can be read out, if required, by the most nervous leader, and understood by the most ignorant member. In addition, we often produce a short list of possible answers (or lines of discussion) to help the leader even further.

So far then, we've seen a progression in the programme. As the meeting begins, the Welcome concentrates on gathering and mingling people together. The Worship then aims to elevate the meeting by glorifying God in praise and prayer. The word 'glorify' literally means 'to make great', and our aim here is to fill the gathering with a great and certain sense of God's presence. That prepares us to receive his word to us with an emphasis on our spiritual growth. And that leads us directly to the final part, the Witness section. Here, the assumption is that the more we feel ourselves growing as Christians, the more we'll see the need for going out from the cell meeting and applying what we've learned in the world outside. As the group moves systematically through the four Ws, there's a natural progression—gathering, glorifying, growing and then going.

Witness

This section is very practical. It's there as a reminder that everything we learn from God needs applying and working out in down-to-earth ways. It may begin with a time of prayer and ministry for each other, based on what we've just been learning. But it will always end by focusing outwards and reminding us of the call to go. To facilitate this, cell members are encouraged to keep what's often called an *oikos* list. The word *oikos* meant 'household' in the New Testament. What it can mean today is our network of friends, family, colleagues and neighbours—in other words the people closest to us in terms of relationships.

In the cell, people are encouraged to identify two or three particular people whom we want God to bless, and particularly ones whom they desire would come to faith. In other words, there's a recognition here that although God cares about everyone, he often puts particular people on our hearts to encourage us in our witness. So the cell provides a place and opportunity to follow our hearts. To back this up, the group commits itself not only to praying, but actually to planning events that will build bridges into those people's lives. For instance, the group may plan a barbecue and invite their non-Christian partners or friends. Or they may meet a practical need like helping somebody move house. Or they may decide to invite people to a mission or a concert or a service. What's important is that all these possibilities are talked about and planned within the group in the context of prayer. And that, in a nutshell, is Witness.

In the following chapters I'll return to the four Ws diet. I'll also talk about additional types of spiritual nutrition that form a vital back-up to the cell structure. But let me end this overview with a glance at the most vital ingredient of all. It's called values.

'You are what you eat!'

I'm not very good when it comes to dieting. I begin with good intentions and make some changes in the amounts I eat, but it's not very long before my family are saying, 'What's that you're eating? Call that a diet? That won't change much!' I soon realize that it's not the quantity I've failed on but the quality. Eating less is no substitute for eating properly, and proper eating requires a little knowledge about nutrition.

In cell church thinking, the single most challenging and encouraging aspect for me is its emphasis on values. In its desire to see the church becoming all that it's meant to be, there are no superficial 'quick fix' ideas. It's not simply a case of doing things more or doing them less, but on doing them properly. 'Never change a structure till you change a value', was a memorable conference phrase that I heard once. Another was, 'We do what we value and value what we do'. And the advice was sensible and sober—don't even think about implementing cell church principles until your church is embracing some key underlying values. Those values have been honed down to five, and I've arranged them in the form of an ABC to make them more memorable. Think of them as vitamins that need to saturate the diet.

- **A**ll involved: every member in ministry;
- **B**ecoming disciples: radically applying and adapting God's word to our lives;
- **C**reating community: not just attending meetings, but sharing lives and building relationships;
- **D**oing evangelism: as opposed to just talking about it;
- **E**ncountering Jesus: expecting a release of his presence and power among his people.

Challenging stuff! Where these values are either weak or non-existent, a church may need to be taught them consistently for up to five years before considering a change in the structures and a move towards cell church. On the other hand, where these values are already present, then cell structures are ideally suited to see them thrive. The million-dollar question is whether and how far we are going to embrace the values, and that question should never be glossed over.

Many of us have watched churches who've caught on to the vision and structures of the latest popular movement, whether it be Alpha, Vineyard, Toronto, Pensacola or whatever, only to see it all end in tears because the underlying values were never embraced. It's so easy to convince ourselves that we believe in something and yet be blind to the full picture. Imagine, for instance, a church that teaches the concept of every-member ministry. Every member in the church is well versed in what it means and Mrs Average is no exception. She accepts it and talks about it and even runs her own house group. But when she goes into hospital and receives a visit from the care team instead of the vicar, you soon discover that her actual values are not the ones she talked about! She loves the idea of a role in the church, but hates it when the vicar's role stops him from giving her a personal pastoral call.

In my own spiritual journey I've had to deal at times with a little 'trapped fat'—assumptions about how churches should operate that have sometimes obscured and confused my grasp of important values. That 'cellulite tendency' is there in us all, but how can we get rid of it? As we move through the next few chapters, I'd like us to re-examine our values and get some fresh ideas for getting into shape. Each chapter will focus on one of the five values I've listed. As we unpack them, let's be honest about the extent to which we feed on each of these values. And remember, 'You are what you eat!'

Cell outline

Welcome

How do you try and stay healthy and keep in shape? (In particular, mention anything that is painless and fun!)

Worship

Reflect together on the need to keep in shape spiritually. Read aloud the following verses allowing a few moments reflection between each one: Romans 12:11; Galatians 5:25; Ephesians 4:3; Ephesians 6:18; 2 Timothy 1:13; 2 Timothy 4:5; Hebrews 13:1; Hebrews 13:5; 1 John 5:21; Jude 1:21. Respond in prayer to what has been read, confessing where you are weak and asking God for his strength.

Word

Reflect together on what you've read in this chapter under the following headings:

- **Choosing the right plan:** On a scale of 1 to 10, how much priority do you feel home groups get in the life of your church compared to other activities (such as services, organizations and other regular events)?
- **Cutting out and cutting down:** Are there areas in your own life or in the church's life that you feel challenged to consider pruning?
- **Sticking to the diet:** Invite each person to share what they find attractive or unappealing about the four Ws structure.
- **'You are what you eat':** Discuss what you value most together in the life of your church. How many of the five cell church values would you openly embrace together? Which would you highlight as the strongest and the weakest at the moment?

Witness

A key feature of a cell group is its willingness to focus outwards in practical ways. I mentioned in particular *oikos* lists and social events. Would you be willing as a group to explore these further? If so here are two suggestions.

1. Agree to go away and write a list of your immediate network of contacts and in particular the people you would like the group to pray for. Make an agreement to share one or two names at your next meeting, and to pray specifically for those people over the next few weeks.

2. Using Appendix 3 as a list of ideas, begin to plan a simple event to which you could happily invite one or two people.
   • Pray together for the idea you've agreed on, and pray also about anything you don't yet feel comfortable with.
   • Pray that you will receive together a common vision for the future.
   • Pray especially for your leader, thanking God for their willingness to serve, and ask that they might be specially encouraged through the next few weeks of reflection.

Chapter 3

Value No 1: All Involved

'Teacher,' they said, 'there is something we want you to do for us.' 'What is it?' Jesus asked them. They answered, 'When you sit on your throne in your glorious kingdom, we want you to let us sit with you, one at your right and one at your left.'

MARK 10:35–37 (GNB)

I've always felt a lot of sympathy for James and John. If we're honest, we're just like them. Caught up in the joy and excitement of knowing Jesus, we often want to get closer. We want to be on the right and the left where the action is, where all the power and the mercy and grace are released. The trouble is that whenever someone else seems to take those places, we behave more like the other disciples who 'became angry'. We'll return to the anger later but notice that Jesus wasn't angry. Was it because he recognized the limitations of their understanding? Certainly he seemed to accept that they asked in good faith, naively perhaps, but with an innocence and sincerity that many of us start out with in our heart of hearts. So he didn't rebuke them for wanting to bask in his glory or share in his greatness. What he did do, however, was to challenge their understanding of greatness:

So Jesus called them all together to him and said, 'You know that the men who are considered rulers of the heathen have power over them, and the leaders have complete authority. This, however, is not the way it is among you. If one of you wants to be great, he must be the servant of the rest; and if one of you wants to be first, he must be the slave of all. For even the Son of Man did not come to be served; he came to serve and to give his life to redeem many people.' (Mark 10:42–45, GNB)

In this chapter I want to outline how cell-based churches aim to encourage a genuine atmosphere of service and equal partnership, where every member is valued and involved.

When I first arrived in Haydock, I'd have described St Mark's as a 'James and John' type church. I don't mean that everybody was competing for greatness, but that people only placed value on one or two roles and titles. The problem for James and John was that they naturally assumed that the 'right' and 'left' positions were the best, and perhaps the only ones that guaranteed a piece of the action. In the same way, St Mark's had a tendency to perceive only three roles as important ones—the vicar, the wardens and the lay readers. Beyond that, there were one or two heads of departments, like the Sunday school, but nobody else got a look in. What's more, the community itself had a very strong 'bosses and workers' mentality. In the early 1900s Haydock had been a thriving mining community, and stories abound of how the mine managers would 'lord it' over their employees, even to the extent of 'persuading' them which church they should attend! St Mark's was born and built on the values of this prevailing culture and it took many years to change from being status centred to more service oriented. Things have steadily changed, but it took a simple cell-based strategy to see a real transformation and mobilization of all its members. Before I explain that strategy, let's just reflect on what we find in most of our churches when it comes to gifting and involvement.

First of all, there's a tendency for many of our gifts to be *undervalued*. This is probably not surprising when you take into account the human condition: most of us spend our time looking for the obviously and naturally gifted, the 'equipped and ready to roll' types, the confident, the top man for the job. But the world just isn't like that. Not only did Jesus recognize this but he emphasized it in his choice of disciples. Surely out of the crowd available he could have chosen some relatively compatible and well-adjusted natural leaders? Instead, he seemed to go out of his way to emphasize and demonstrate what a fallen world tends to offer by way of gifts and what God can do in response. Somebody once passed on to me this imaginary memo:

To: Jesus, son of Joseph, Woodcrafter, Carpenter's Shop, Nazareth
From: Jordan Management Consultants, Jerusalem

Dear Sir

Thank you for submitting the résumés of the twelve men you have picked for management positions in your new organization. All of them have now taken our battery of tests; we have not only run the results through our computer, but have also arranged personal interviews for each of them with our psychologist and vocational aptitude consultant. It is the staff opinion that most of your nominees are lacking in background, education and vocational aptitude for the type of enterprise you are undertaking. For a start, they do not have the team concept. We would recommend that you continue your search for persons of experience in managerial ability and proven capability.

Simon Peter is emotionally unstable and given to fits of temper. Andrew has absolutely no qualities of leadership. The two brothers, James and John, the sons of Zebedee, place personal interest above company loyalty. Thomas demonstrates a questioning attitude that would tend to undermine morale. We feel it is our duty to tell you that Matthew has been blacklisted by the greater Jerusalem Better Business Bureau. James, son of Alphaeus, and Thaddaeus definitely have radical leanings, and they both registered a high score on the manic-depressive scale.

One of the candidates, however, shows great potential. He is a man of ability and resourcefulness and meets people well, has a keen business mind and has contacts in high places. He is highly motivated and very ambitious. We recommend Judas Iscariot as your controller and right-hand man.

All of the other profiles are self-explanatory. We wish you success in your new venture.

Why do we so often fail to see 'success' in our ministry ventures? Is it perhaps because we start out with the wrong expectations? If Jesus found that he was still dealing with as much immaturity, incompetence, pride and lack of faith at the end of his ministry as at the beginning, why should we expect more? I love the motto that somebody gave me at the beginning of my ministry and that I've held on to ever since: 'Jesus came only for failures'. In his kingdom there's a healthy expectation that we're dealing with very raw material, and raw material takes time and patience to process. Jesus, however, didn't wait for the finished product. He took weak and fallible human beings and started taking risks. He went out of his way, in fact, to draw out the very people that others would overlook. Teaching about grace, he'd immediately put the spotlight on a Zacchaeus or a woman of Bethany in order to emphasize the potential of all, and especially the despised and rejected. Later on, the naturally gifted and multi-talented Paul went to great pains to share what he'd learnt, that 'God chose the weak things of the world to shame the strong' (1 Corinthians 1:27). Despite his talent, he insisted, 'If I must boast, I will boast of the things that show my weakness' (2 Corinthians 11:30). In dealing with others he began with the principle that 'we who are strong ought to bear with the failings of the weak and not to please ourselves' (Romans 15:1). And he testified proudly of God's specific word to him, that 'my power is made perfect in weakness' (2 Corinthians 12:9). The Living Bible puts it in a form that could become a cell church slogan: 'My strength shows up best in weak people.'

All leaders and ministers are surrounded by weak people, including themselves, but every book in scripture reverberates with the truth that God delights in drawing out potential. Over the years I've been amazed at the transformation I've seen in seemingly ungifted and unconfident people. Twelve years ago, a lady in our church came to see me. She was short in stature and very short on confidence, so much so that she stood at the door shaking like a leaf, wondering how on earth to communicate with her new vicar. Twelve years on and the same lady now heads up our communication team. She administrates, negotiates and even mediates and does it with grace, humility and a God-given poise. Fifteen years ago, her husband was a hard-drinking, hard-gambling working man. His favourite taunt was that all Christian men were women (till a young lad broke his nose in a church rugby match!). Today that same man is a cell pastor and a core leader in the church, and his main passion and gifting is in ministering to men! I believe his most moving moment came after ministering to 50 Anglican clergymen at a conference in Tanzania. Working alongside me, he befriended them, encouraged and prayed with them, shared his insights and led a small group. In a time of testimony at the end of the conference one of them publicly paid tribute to him as 'the gifted man of God'. It reduced him to tears.

God delights in taking undervalued, unconfident and seemingly untalented people, and turning them into effective ministers. That's why we should never look at our churches and say there's no talent, no leadership and no potential there. It may take time to develop and emerge, but it comes in special doses in the kingdom of God. What's needed, of course, is an effective model for nurturing gifts and encouraging people so that all can be involved, and that's where a cell group comes into its own. Ministry begins when the weakest people find an environment where they can take the smallest step to healing and greater confidence. It continues when that step is followed by another and another and another until valuable and practical gifts emerge. What better environment than the small group to encourage such a process?

The second thing we need to recognize about our gifts is that they're often *under the surface*. Recently I managed to fulfil a lifelong ambition. At home I have an aquarium of live corals and marine fish, and I've always wanted to swim on a real coral reef. This summer my opportunity came. Setting out by boat off the Florida Keys, we sailed out to sea in a straight line for about five miles. By the time we reached the reef there was no sign of land and little sign of life. It was one of those moments when you could have played 'I spy' with the letter S—sun, sea and sky! We then received some instruction and slipped head down into the water equipped with mask and fins. The underwater world that suddenly appeared was absolutely breath-taking. Immediately we were surrounded by teeming shoals of multi-coloured fish of every conceivable shape and size, and all against a living backdrop of algaes, sea anemones and waving corals. It was another world on another level, a phenomenal experience I'll never forget.

Getting back to home, I can see a parallel here with the world of church. Often we can walk among our congregations and it can feel like that empty sea. Where are the leaders, the gifts and commitment? How can we possibly begin another new venture when we're struggling to resource the original one? The problem, I believe, is that we look at our situation on the wrong level. We see things as they are on the surface and we get discouraged. The experts tell us that what we need is a 'paradigm shift': we need to take our eyes off the empty sea and dive under the surface. It's a small enough action, but it radically shifts our whole perspective and the way we view our landscape. Once we do it, we suddenly see a shoal of opportunities for releasing people's gifts in all kinds of areas.

Let's use a practical example. Let's assume that a church has been trying to make the shift to every-member ministry. It already has a rota of pray-ers and readers for the Sunday services, but the list is looking a little depleted. One or two people have dropped out and the others are feeling overused. The next step, then, is to go through the membership list, but although we know most of the people on it, we can't possibly be aware of everyone's full potential or availability, so we draw a blank. Next we might give out a few notices requesting help and asking for volunteers. That may bring one or two gifted people on board (as well as a few unhelpful and ungifted ones!), but in my experience the majority don't respond. When you ask them why, they all have similar reasons: 'We thought lots of other people would volunteer'; 'We don't have the confidence'; 'We prefer to be asked personally'. What we need at this stage is to see the situation on a whole new level and from a different perspective.

Week by week, the cell members have been learning to read the Bible and pray together, and one or two of the shy, unconfident ones are now contributing. So when a memo is passed to the cell leaders requesting names for the pray-ers and readers rota, something begins to happen. First of all, the need is shared and the whole group becomes involved in the selection. Together they tackle the request and together they can nominate people for selection—after all, they're the ones who hear each other read and pray each week! This does two things: firstly it alters the vicar's role as the sole talent-spotter and makes all the church members more accountable and involved in meeting the church's needs. And secondly, it allows hidden and emerging gifts to be easily identified and encouraged into the wider forum. To conclude on this point, let me say I've been teaching the principles of every-member ministry for the last seventeen years, but the shift to a cell-based model has meant all the difference between admiring an aquarium and accessing the sea—there's no comparison!

The third thing that we often find about our gifts is that they're *unfairly categorized*. We so easily attach a greater importance to some ministries than others, and again it was no different in Paul's day. Writing to the Romans he said, 'Do not think of yourself more highly than you ought, but rather think of yourself with sober judgment, in accordance with the measure of faith God has given you. Just as each of us has one body with many members, and these members do not all have the same function, so in Christ we who are many form one body, and each member belongs to all the others' (Romans 12:3–5).

Imagine walking by a lake when suddenly you hear screams and see someone drowning. You dive in, swim across the lake and grab the person. But now, ask yourself which part of the body was most important in performing the rescue. Was it the ear that heard the cry? Or was it the eye that saw the person drowning? Or could it be the legs that ran towards the lake or the arms that swam or the hand that reached out? Of course, the answer is that all of them were vital and it'd be ridiculous to single out any one of them.

One of the aspects of cell that I love is the way that it spreads responsibility and emphasizes many equal parts. I've always believed in shared ministry but have often felt uncomfortable with the way we've gone about labelling our leaders. The word 'elder', for instance, carries all kinds of connotations, some of which emphasize a setting apart and can even suggest a setting above. A cell church model, on the other hand, draws many into leadership and shares the load more evenly. A cell leader will never have more than fifteen members to care for and as soon as possible will have an assistant. That leadership is then supported by a network of cell pastors (often called supervisors, although I prefer not to use the word). Again they will only be asked to relate to four or five groups, and their role is actually far more supportive than supervisory (which is why I don't use the word). For churches that grow a larger number of cells, an area pastor is appointed to mentor the leaders. In churches with 100 to 150 members, this would be the vicar or senior pastor. As the church grows, however, this role is shared and divided too, and is often a full-time appointment. In all this, there is a distinct sense of consistently spreading the load, sharing the ministry and serving the whole.

It's interesting that Jethro recognized that when he advised Moses in Exodus 18. The story highlights Moses' exhaustion and isolation as a leader, but it also emphasizes practical service over leadership hierarchy. Jethro suggested a very practical spreading of leadership over thousands, hundreds, fifties and tens, very similar to a cell model. He then said, 'Select capable men from all the people' (Exodus 18:21). In other words he looked to the whole body, to all the people, to meet the criteria for leadership. He didn't look for the ones who were officially qualified or well connected. They had to be 'capable', but in Jethro's words that simply meant 'trustworthy men who hate dishonest gain'.

In a cell-based church, the word 'leader' gets used a lot more often for a lot more people, but it doesn't mean 'boss'. It means a person who's emerged as 'trustworthy' when it comes to serving others and ministering to the whole. That's a very liberating thought for those of us who are constantly on the lookout for new leaders. Too often we look for the articulate and the influential and in some churches they simply don't seem to exist. Choosing leaders should be far more about looking for people who genuinely love their fellow cell members and who have a servant heart. The person who is faithful and attentive in those areas can be taught how to facilitate a small group far more easily than the over-confident characters who love the sound of their own voice.

Remember, too, that any prospective cell leader is never thrown in at the deep end, but is gradually encouraged into the role with the hands-on support of the cell pastor. Wherever they are weak, they are not only offered advice and training, but encouraged to ask others in the cell to help them and share the load. In this way, a cell leader is not seen as an authority figure driving the group, but rather as a servant who enables and releases others.

The fourth thing I'd want to say about our gifts is that they're often left *unclaimed*. For several years as a roving singer and evangelist I used to travel frequently by air, often going through the tedious process of passport control and baggage collection that many of us encounter on package holidays. I used to stand there, watching the conveyor belt going round and round, and rather too often I'd still be there half an hour later because my baggage had been lost! Over the years I became a professional baggage observer, but what really used to intrigue me was that long after the crowds had disappeared, there were still one or two suitcases lying on the conveyor belt unclaimed. They obviously belonged to someone, and presumably were needed, but they were never picked up and carried away. As I stood there thinking about the owners of all these bags and why they'd not collected them, it made me think about the church's unclaimed baggage. The Bible promises that every Christian can be gifted and equipped by God, but very often the gifts are left unclaimed and unopened. Why does that happen?

Back in the baggage hall, I used to come up with three reasons. Either people assumed that someone else had taken the bags, or they forgot about them, or they expected someone else to do the collecting. In the church it's often the same. First of all, our gifts and ministries can be taken by others. Too often, the same few people are doing several jobs in the church and it's impossible for the newcomer to find a role. Secondly, gifts and ministries are forgotten or simply never thought about in the first place. Four or five years into the Christian life and some of us forget that we were meant to be carrying any bags. Others have been carrying a particular ministry bag for the last fifteen years and have never recognized that there are other bags to collect. My first five years at St Mark's were spent convincing some wonderful servants that God didn't necessarily give us one ministry for life. Some of us can be labouring so faithfully in a single ministry that we lose sight of the God of new things who constantly moves us on and moves others in. And thirdly, there are those who always expect someone else to collect the gifts, as the following little story suggests.

This story concerns four people—everybody, somebody, anybody and nobody. There was an important job to be done, and everybody was asked to do it. Anybody could have done it, but in the end nobody did it. Somebody got very angry over this because it was really everybody's job. Everybody thought anybody would do it, but nobody realized that everybody wouldn't do it. And it ended up that everybody blamed somebody when actually nobody had asked anybody. The body of Christ in action!

The problem of unclaimed baggage is a problem of expectations and communication. Nobody is very sure what's required of them, and those who do know don't communicate it. Communication has always been a headache in the church, especially for leaders, but cells provide an ideal vehicle for clarifying and communicating all kinds of issues. Over a period of time, all cell members will know that their gifts are valued and will be used. They'll also be aware that information flows freely and frequently between cell members, leaders, and pastors, and that a list of gifts required and gifts on offer will constantly be exchanged. In time, the need for church notices diminishes then disappears as the cells stay connected.

I recently visited a cell church in Hong Kong that has no church building. It has nine Sunday congregations to choose from and each one meets in six different venues over a two-month period. They simply move around the whole community, quite literally bringing the church to the people! That kind of strategy would be a nightmare in the traditional fellowship, but a cell-based church will communicate what it's doing and where it's meeting through its members from week to week. If someone misses a cell meeting, the leader will call and keep them up to date. Through cells, the bags are all collected and Christians stay connected.

All for one and one for all

In cell-based churches there isn't much room for the multi-talented star who takes on the world and the church almost single-handedly. Instead there is a genuine commitment to work together for the common good and, like the musketeers, members have a real sense of 'all for one and one for all'. Let's be specific and list some of the ways in which cell groups aim to get 'all involved'.

Meetings

Cell groups have a specific strategy to involve every member in the running of a meeting. First of all, there's often a policy to use as many available homes as possible. This may not always be appropriate but it can stimulate the life of a cell in several ways. It gives more people the opportunity and privilege of opening their own homes and discovering the gift of hospitality. That in turn takes a little pressure off the leader who now only needs to prepare for the meeting and doesn't have to think about preparing his or her home. Where babysitting is a problem, it can take a little pressure off young families if the parents don't have to leave the house. In another situation it can encourage the single person (particularly older folk) who may not have so many opportunities to share their home with others. One of our cells, for instance, deliberately meets most of the time in the home of an elderly widow. She loves to open her home and relishes the 'grandmother' role, while the cell relishes an endless supply of delicious buns and cakes! In yet another situation, it can occasionally be good to meet in a home where there's an unchurched partner. Often it can help to build relationships and bridges with the person who now gets to meet Christians outside the church context and on his or her own turf. Every cell member's situation will be very different, but the conscious aim is to spread around the opportunity for offering hospitality.

In the meeting itself, the load is consciously shared. Because the meeting has four clear sections, parts of it can easily be delegated to other members of the cell. It may be that only one or two feel confident enough to do this, but as they offer themselves they always find some helpful suggestions and encouragement from the cell outline notes that are provided. In time, it becomes increasingly obvious who should now be invited to become an assistant leader, and that person in time will inherit their own group when the cell multiplies. Every member contributes in some way—reading the scriptures, leading in prayer, keeping a cell diary, organizing social events and so on. In cell groups, the leader is neither expected nor allowed to carry the whole programme. But who, then, ensures that happens and how do the leaders stay accountable?

Leadership

An encouraging aspect of cell-based ministry is the sense of mutual accountability across the whole life of the church. As cell leaders, cell pastors and area pastors meet together in different contexts on a regular basis, communication flows freely in all directions. News and needs are shared, new ideas are passed on, problems are grappled with and constructive appraisal given. On the one hand, a cell pastor will meet with leaders individually and help them appraise their own ministry (see Appendix 1). On the other hand the vicar will be told where the cell outlines are hitting the mark, and when they're over-complicated, confusing or simply boring! In different churches the pattern and frequency of meetings will differ widely but in all cases the principles of accountability and communication are taken very seriously.

All this may begin to sound a little prescriptive and restricting, but as the leader of a growing church I've found it extremely liberating. In the past there were times when I used to feel paralysed by a sense of pastoral unawareness. Once I had reached my own personal capacity to communicate with individuals, I was then only left with the voice of rumour: 'people are saying this', or 'everybody's feeling that', and 'we can't say who's saying it, but…'. Busy pastors can become so snowed under and so unconnected that it becomes impossible to discern truth from rumour, especially when the flak begins to fly! Cells have changed all that, and although we're now approaching 600 members, I've never felt more connected to my congregation. How does it work? Very simply, the cell pastors visit each of their four cells over four weeks, and every four weeks will meet with me. They meet with me in other contexts but once a month they will specifically feed back the information or issues that they feel I ought to know about, or that the cell members want me to know. From that, they will help me discern where my time and energy should be spent, and they support me as I try to be accountable for my own ministry. They in turn are accountable to me, and they model the same kind of relationship with each of their cell leaders.

To understand more clearly how leaders relate in this context, let me try and define the difference between a cell leader and cell pastor. A *cell leader*'s role is primarily pastoral, with a little organization thrown in. Although they need to acquire some basic skills in group leading, they aren't meant to be Bible teachers, preachers or counsellors. Whenever the groups gather, most of the material is provided and the leaders concentrate on being facilitators. In other words, they give away as much of the ministry as possible to the other members and coordinate the results. Their major role is to be carers. Week by week they build personal relationships with each of the members. Outside the meeting, they will aim to have contact with every person through the week. It may simply be a chat after a service or a short phone call, but every member is looked out for, cared for and prayed for regularly by the cell leader.

The *cell pastor*'s role is threefold. First, they again have a pastoral role. Their main aim is to support and encourage the cell leaders in any way possible. That may well include occasionally leading the cell, but theirs is mainly a background back-up ministry. Whenever a cell is struggling or a member is in need, the pastor is at hand to help. In that sense, a cell leader never walks alone. Second, the cell pastors have a major role in communication. Not only will they pass anything important in the life of the cell to the leadership, but anything of importance in the life of the church will be brought by them into each of the cells. And finally, the cell pastor is concerned with quality control. They encourage the leaders and their assistants to follow cell principles and keep to the programme and guidelines. Again, this is not a one-way process. If the leaders feel that too much is required of them or they're facing a difficult time, the cell pastor's main purpose is to encourage, enable and serve. In this way, a bond develops between leader and pastor, where roles are seen as complementary rather than hierarchical. In the end, it's this kind of mutual support, along with responsibility in fairly small doses, that allows the church to grow more leaders over a shorter period. No one is ever thrown in at the deep end but everybody is stretched and encouraged to grow.

Growing the young

It would be a huge mistake to think that cell-based churches are purely adult-focused. Additional creativity may be needed in ministering to young people through the cell model, but our values become meaningless if they don't apply to the youngest member. There are several possible models that cell churches can adopt. Many will begin by adapting the existing children's programme, with the emphasis on becoming far more relational and pastoral. Groups will be kept small and teaching will be interactive and discussion-based. Children are not simply encouraged to learn the Bible but to learn how to share their needs and experiences and to pray for one another. In fact every value described in this book is worked on and applied at a child's level.

Another interesting model is the intergenerational cell. These are very much in their infancy in this country, but effectively draw the whole family together in fellowship, from the youngest child to the oldest grandparent. Again, the format of the meeting itself is adapted, but it always begins with all-age icebreakers and worship. Sometimes, the children leave at that point, and the adults take it in turns to play aunt and uncle in another room! The children then return for the Witness section and pray with the cell. Obviously, the logistics differ according to the make-up of the group, but this kind of cell values all-age ministry very highly.

A model that is now being widely introduced in this country is the peer-led youth cell. These are particularly exciting, as the teenagers themselves lead the groups and are stretched into leadership early on.

In this situation, the existing older youth leader becomes the cell pastor, training and supporting but staying away from most of the cell meetings. The structure and content remain the same, but the young people themselves adapt and modify the material to suit that particular group. On a personal level, I've been stunned to watch the rate at which my own seventeen-year-old son (now nineteen) grew from being an unconfident adolescent to a visionary leader! Each week he works at his material, making it simple, challenging and direct. He then phones round all the members and makes sure they're coming. It's been uncanny at times to see a mirror image of myself as leader. Some weeks he appears dejected and discouraged, having had a tough evening. Often, though, he's excited and delighted at the way God has used him and his sixteen-year-old co-leader. Although he values the support of his twenty-something cell pastor, they never feel it's the same when an adult is present! In fact, stories now abound of the way peer-led youth cells are growing and multiplying across the whole country. Meanwhile, we run a variation on the theme with our eleven- to fourteen-year-olds. Emerging out of childhood, they are now learning to follow a normal cell format but still led by an adult. Read their testimonies in Chapter 9. The impression is not so much of children as of emerging leaders. The future is secure!

Servant ministry

Not everyone is a leader, but everyone can play a vital part in the ministry. In the following chapters, we'll see how every member can be mobilized in evangelism, pastoral care and prayer ministry. In fact, there's really no area of church life where you can't see 'all involved'. For example, there are jobs that few people enjoy doing on their own (with the exception of a few true servant types!). These are the roll-your-sleeves-up, background-type jobs—shifting hundreds of chairs before a major event, acres of carpet cleaning afterwards, or the churchyard that's threatening to turn into the *Day of the Triffids*! Asking for volunteers on these occasions can go down like a lead balloon in the most enlightened of fellowships. When it becomes part of our cell life, however, the dynamic is quite different. No longer are we being asked to volunteer single-handedly, never knowing whether anyone else will turn up. Suddenly it's become a community activity and a very tangible demonstration of cell life.

At St Mark's, we do this in two ways. Where there are several special church events over the year, two or three cells will cover each event. Once or twice a year, they will serve as a group, organizing chairs, refreshments and clearing up. Doing it in this way, they see it as part of their mission as well as an expression of their life together. Again no one is asked to take on too much but everyone is invited to take a turn. We have another occasion once a year when all the cells turn up to spring-clean the whole church. Over a two-week period, we ask each of the cells to give an evening (in place of their meeting), and to arrive at the church armed with dusters, paint-brushes, mops, brooms and spades. They then have a choice of working parties to join, and can either paint, clean, dig or make the tea. Being a servant in this context is not only fun, but an important step in learning to get on board in giving and service. It also helps us to see each other as normal people, capable of holding a brush as well as a hymn book!

Speaking of hymn books, the Sunday service presents a number of servant roles that again can be coordinated through the cells. At each service, books need giving out, people need welcoming, tea needs making, prayers leading and the scriptures read. At St Mark's, we now give all these roles to the cells on a rota basis. Every few months they will plan who is going to do what and encourage and pray for each other. Some may feel nervous as they're asked to read or lead the prayers in church for the very first time, but they come away with a deep sense of corporate achievement and mutual encouragement. In the same service, the cell pastor will welcome the congregation and sometimes introduce a testimony from the cell. In this way, the larger church is introduced to its wider leadership on a regular basis. Of course, this particular model is only appropriate in large churches where responsibility can be shared among many cells, but the principle of total involvement can be applied in the smallest fellowship and still coordinated through its cell life.

Mission

We must never forget that every church member can be a missionary. A typical cell can personally adopt a missionary or mission agency and become involved in practical support—raising funds, sending gifts, writing letters and so on. A particular feature in many larger cell-based churches, however, is an increasing emphasis on mobilizing the cell itself. In an overseas church I visited recently, 60 per cent of its 1200 membership had all been involved in short-term (two-week) missions. Many other churches manage to encourage one cell member in every group to do this. The group itself supports them by prayer, planning and finance. This is something we're beginning to see at St Mark's, and it goes without saying that there's a massive difference between occasionally hearing a missionary mentioned in prayer, and encouraging one of our very own cell members in their first overseas venture. Apart from individual support, we now use a proportion of our mission budget for this greater mobilization of the body.

Vision

Leaders often like to think that God has blessed them with fairly fertile minds and a creative spirit. But the greater blessing comes from involving the whole church in the visionary process. Shared leadership takes matters like consensus and consultation for granted, but it's easy for churches to come unstuck at times of major change and development. How do we ensure that everyone understands the vision? Can we be sure they'll support it? Where are the weaknesses and what else should be considered? Whenever our church has been on the move again, I've always tried to consult and involve, but the cells have added a whole new dimension. When a major project is introduced, the vision is shared with the whole church, beginning with all the leaders. In fact the leaders help to sharpen it and smooth out the rough edges before it's shared more widely. But then the cells take it away and become part of the process. Together they talk and pray about it, then feed back their comments, anxieties, questions and suggestions. In this way, the whole body is involved through the whole process. In fact some of the most important questions and issues arise directly out of the cell groups' input. Not all of us dream the dreams, but we all play a vital part in making them a reality.

All or nothing?

Coming back to James and John, the focus shifts in that story from their request to the disciples' response: 'When the other ten disciples heard about it, they became angry with James and John (Mark 10:4, GNB). Why were they angry? And why is it that we often react in the same way? The question of roles, titles, positions and responsibilities arises involving the few, and the rest react angrily. It may not be expressed publicly, but at times the church may appear to be rife with jealousy, bitterness, pride and fear. People who once offered everything are now offering nothing. To use one of our leader's favourite expressions, 'They've taken their ball home'!

Sometimes the issue is *jealousy*: I've been excluded. Other people have put themselves on the right and left of Jesus and now there's no room for me. The jobs, the positions and the limelight have all been taken and I'm left on the outside. Or the problem may be *bitterness*: I've been hurt. The people who've taken those positions are the very same people who hurt me, and they don't deserve to be at Jesus' side because they sinned against me. Or the issue may be *pride*: I've been underestimated. They've allowed those two to position themselves and they don't realize that I'm better qualified. Or there might be a problem of *fear*: I've been overlooked. They're all talking about James and John and nobody ever talks about me. I'm so insignificant and that makes me afraid of who I am. It also makes me angry about who they think they are. They don't realize how it feels to be overlooked.

How could Jesus possibly be angry with James and John when in fact all the disciples needed healing? They simply needed to hear again the words, 'Do not be afraid, little flock, for your Father has been pleased to give you the kingdom' (Luke 12:32). There's no doubt that life in cells has a pleasing way of giving involvement to all in a practical and dynamic way. It also gets to grips with some of these deeper issues that affect the flock, and I want to look at those next.

Cell outline

Welcome

If you could change places with a Bible character for a day, who would you choose, and why?

Worship

Brainstorm a list of all the ministries, organizations and jobs in your church (however small) and write them down. Focus your worship on thanking God specifically for the people who are serving in all those areas. Begin by reading aloud 1 Corinthians 12:4—11, then take it in turns to pray thanksgiving prayers for all the areas and people you have mentioned. Give space for silence, but also read small portions of scripture from the rest of the chapter to feed people's reflections and inspire further prayer.

Word

Read Mark 10:35–45.

1. If you had been one of the disciples, how might you have been tempted to react to James and John? For example:
   - jealousy: 'They've excluded me'
   - bitterness: 'They've hurt me'
   - pride: 'They've underestimated me'
   - fear: 'They've overlooked me'

2. Would you agree that our gifts can sometimes be:
   - undervalued?
   - under the surface?
   - unfairly categorized?
   - unclaimed?

Spend a few minutes talking about times you have found that to be true in the church, then share one or two testimonies of how people's gifts have been discovered, encouraged and used to the full.

3. Are there any practical ideas in this chapter that fire your imagination for involving every person in your church?

Witness

- Begin to follow up the things you discussed and planned during your last meeting.
- Talk for a few minutes about how you might spread responsibility for the overall running of your group.
- Pray for the involvement of every Christian in your fellowship, and pray specifically for each other's involvement—for those who feel involved and have a role, and for those who don't and perhaps wonder where they fit in. Remember that, for some people, their major role is in the workplace, and they may have very little time to be involved inside the fellowship.

Chapter 4

Value No 2: Becoming Disciples

Now when he saw the crowds, he went up on a mountainside and sat down. His disciples came to him, and he began to teach them.
MATTHEW 5:1

Whenever I read the Sermon on the Mount it always makes me think of Bible weeks like Keswick and New Wine. Situated in beautiful surroundings, the people pour in from all around and soak themselves in teaching from the cream of the country's preachers. I imagine the disciples sat there enraptured. In fact it says they 'were amazed at his teaching, because he taught as one who had authority, and not as their teachers of the law' (7:28–29). I imagine some of the whispered comments like, 'My rabbi never preaches like this'; 'It's about time we had some deeper teaching'; 'Now this is what I call solid food'. But almost as if Jesus senses what they're thinking, he suddenly switches gear towards the end and drives home his challenge: 'Why do you call me Lord, Lord and do not do what I say?' (Luke 6:46). The fact is that it's far easier to talk about learning than live out what we've learnt.

Don't get me wrong—I think Bible weeks have a really important place in making disciples, but as a pastor I've sometimes felt saddened and frustrated at some of the long-term effects. You know the kind of scenario, where people return on a high and give glowing testimonies, then within a couple of months they hit the rocks again, or simply slide slowly back into a spiritual mire. Some churches lay a commendable emphasis on the importance of teaching and preaching and yet inadvertently end up with a spiritual spoon-feeding culture. A stirring sermon on Sunday morning is followed by an in-depth exposition on Sunday night. The midweek top-up comes in the form of a Bible study and prayer meeting, then the week ends off with a rally and a visiting preacher before the cycle begins all over again. The problem with this approach is twofold. First, there is no way of telling whether the teaching has actually been understood and received. And secondly, depth of Bible knowledge is often mistaken for depth of maturity. It's interesting that when we talk about 'solid food', we take the phrase straight out of the book of Hebrews, where the writer says, 'Though by this time you ought to be teachers, you need someone to teach you the elementary truths of God's word all over again. You need milk, not solid food' (Hebrews 5:12).

When we think of a teacher, we think of somebody standing at the front with Bible in hand. But this was written to the Jews, and their tradition took it for granted that a teacher (or rabbi) didn't just preach and feed information to the people. Rather, he modelled what he was teaching and the disciples would have to commit themselves to the man as well as the message. A disciple, then, was someone who was learning to live the life his teacher lived. Bearing that in mind, the writer here is saying that we ought by now to be living out these teachings for others to see. We ought to be modelling a Christian lifestyle and teaching by our own example. He reinforces the point by saying, 'But solid food is for the mature, who by constant use have trained themselves to distinguish good from evil' (5:14). The key phrase is 'constant use'. So when he goes on to say, 'Therefore let us leave the elementary teachings about Christ and go on to maturity' (Hebrews 6:1), he's not saying that we should stop thinking about repentance and faith and all the other things he lists. In fact the teaching in Hebrews covers all these issues again and again. He's saying that we should stop talking about it and start doing it. And when we've started doing it, we should talk a little more and then do it even more until we're doing it all the time. In fact, the more we do it, the more humble we'll probably become about our so-called maturity!

Back in Galilee, Jesus had no intention of allowing his followers to wallow in a sea of sermons. Very quickly he gathered the smaller group and poured his life into them. All his teaching was up for discussion and all his training was on the job. They lived and worked so closely together that no weakness was ever hidden and no need was ever missed. Of course their experience with Jesus was unique and never to be repeated, but the early church continued to follow these principles. They still 'devoted themselves to the apostles' teaching' (Acts 2:42), but now 'all the believers were together and had everything in common' (2:44), and 'every day they continued to meet together' (2:46). There was a massive emphasis on working it out together and sharing a common life which went way beyond the superficial meeting of minds to a deeper sharing of hearts. Since then, of course, the church has tried to follow that model with varying degrees of understanding and success. Bible study groups and fellowship events will often emphasize the priority of living and growing together. But what does all that mean in the nitty-gritty of a normal day-to-day life, and how does a cell church aim at maturing people in measurable and meaningful ways?

Firstly we need to consider how truth can be shared. The New Testament emphasizes and celebrates the gifts of preaching and teaching and the importance of inspired communication. It speaks constantly of the way the apostles proclaimed, exhorted, argued, reasoned, persuaded and pleaded. In fact, it uses over 30 different words to emphasize how the message was conveyed. The way truth is communicated is crucial, but then the way it's received and applied is critical, and that's where cells begin to show their effectiveness.

A good sermon will not only inform but inspire and specifically apply itself to the listener's situation. A good cell will enable that person to assess what he's learned and to become accountable in applying it. That's why most cell churches link the main Sunday sermon with the weekly cell study. It gives a clear opportunity for monitoring our response as well as our understanding. It also offers help in responding and, let's face it, most of us need all the help we can get. Sometimes we talk about Christians being two-faced hypocrites, but the fact is that we all wear about four faces. First of all, there's the me that we all know and recognize and deal with every day. Then there's the me that I recognize but manage to hide from you. But then there's another side of me you recognize and yet I'm blind to, and

I'm never going to see that face unless somebody has the courage and compassion to tell me about it and 'speak the truth in love'. And finally, there's yet another face that neither of us can see. This is the face that lurks beneath the surface in our darker natures and has to be revealed by the Holy Spirit. It may be an inner fear that we barely recognize or an anger that festers so deep inside that we've never acknowledged it. Events or relationships in our past can put yet another face on to already complex characters, so there's little room here for a 'just-me-and-my-saviour' type independence. We need each other and God planned it that way. Let's see then, how the plan should work.

'The Truth will set you free'
(John 8:32)

I once saw a poster that had a picture of a rag doll with its head through a mangle. The caption read, 'The truth will set you free, but first it will make you miserable.' We all find the truth uncomfortable at times, and our natural tendency will either be to run away from it or to find convenient forms of cover-up. The sign I once saw hanging in a Swedish pastor's study would make a very appropriate welcome sign over the cell group's door. It said, 'Please leave your mask here.' When we do let go of our masks, we find a room full of like-minded and like-hearted individuals with the same weaknesses and wounds, and the same need for encouragement in fighting the good fight. When it comes to sharing truth, the conversation has to go beyond how we should be living to what we now experience, for that is the only starting point for genuine change. Without the grace to be really honest about ourselves, the positive voice of conviction turns quickly into the nag of condemnation that will drown out the truth. Of course it doesn't all have to be weakness and warfare. For every confession of struggle there's a testimony of grace, and with every tear there are smiles and laughter too. But a cell group learns the true value of words like 'vulnerability', 'honesty', 'reality' and 'encouragement'.

Now let's dig a little deeper. If sharing truth is about sharing weakness, then we need to find practical ways of doing that. The cell group moves in the right direction as it tries to apply the preaching, but then the average cell will only ever go so far in sharing. Jesus too found himself relating to different kinds and sizes of groups. When he wasn't addressing the crowds, he had a wider fellowship of followers, at least 70 of whom he sent out on mission. He then had the smaller cell of twelve disciples, but even within that there were three with whom he shared on a more intimate level. Only Peter, James and John were allowed into the sick room of Jairus' daughter, and only they went with Jesus to the Mount of Transfiguration and the Garden of Gethsemane, intimate moments where the crowds weren't welcome.

All of us develop friendships at different levels and we give them different names, from pal to soulmate. The cell-based church recognizes this and sees the need for a similar pattern inside the church. The outworking of this will differ in different fellowships, but all cell churches will emphasize the need for a cell sponsor or cell partner for those who've newly come to faith. At St Mark's we call this our 'one-to-one' ministry. For one year at least, the sponsor will meet weekly with the new Christian and walk alongside them as they grow in the faith. Their role is not to teach, preach or even counsel, but to encourage, support and serve. The sponsor is usually either the person who invited them to church in the first place, or another cell member who's befriended them from the very beginning. As the new believer follows a simple programme of introductory Bible study, the sponsor is there to talk to and pray with. Any problems, issues or agendas that arise can all be passed on to other appropriate people or leaders. In this way the new believer learns the value of sharing and accountability from the very beginning.

This value of accountable relationships is worked out in various ways and at different levels in different churches. It's interesting that John Wesley founded his movement on a cell-based strategy, but he also formed a second tier of groups to complement the main classes. These groups were much smaller in number and more radical in nature and were known as bands. This is how Wesley laid out the ground rules:

The design of our meeting is to obey that command of God: 'Confess your faults one to another, and pray for one another, that ye may be healed'. To this end we intend to meet once a week, at the least:

- *To come punctually at the hour appointed, without some extraordinary reason.*
- *To begin exactly at the hour, with singing or prayer.*
- *To speak, each of us in order, freely and plainly, the true state of our souls, with the faults we have committed in thought, word or deed, and the temptations we have felt since our last meeting.*
- *To end every meeting with prayer, suited to the state of each person present.*
- *To desire some person among us to speak his own state first, and then to ask the rest, in order, as many and as searching questions as maybe, concerning their state, sins and temptations. Questions to be asked each week were: What known sins have you committed since our last meeting? What temptations have you met with? How were you delivered? What have you thought, said or done of which you doubt whether it be sin or not?*[7]

Put in such bold, uncompromising terms, it's hard to imagine how 21st-century Christians would react to all that. The truth is, however, that many Christians are crying out for such a system and signing up in increasing numbers to a more accountable style of fellowship. One of the more exciting developments at St Mark's in recent days has been the additional introduction of covenant cells. We first introduced these for leaders, and particularly for the men, as a kind of supplementary diet to encourage personal growth. Sharing and vulnerability don't sit easily or come very naturally in our northern working men's macho society. However, the offer of a simple tool has opened the dam gates in recent days and our men are now sharing! Very simply, we printed a card of self-examination questions, small enough to slip inside a Bible. The questions are very specific and practical and make it very easy to avoid cover-up. They also make an excellent little teaching tool. They illustrate how far we all still have to go and how we all quite clearly stand in the very same place when it comes to spiritual issues—at the foot of the cross. Here are the questions:

- Am I consciously or unconsciously creating the impression that I'm a better person than I really am? In other words, am I a hypocrite?
- Am I honest in all my acts or words, or do I exaggerate?
- Do I confidentially pass on to another what was told to me in confidence?
- Can I be trusted?
- Am I a slave to work, friendships, hobbies or habits?
- Am I self-conscious, self-pitying or self-justifying?
- Did the Bible live for me today?
- Do I give it time to speak to me every day?
- Am I enjoying prayer?
- When did I last speak to somebody else about Jesus?
- Am I making contacts with other people and using them for the kingdom?
- Do I pray about the money I spend?
- Do I get to bed in time and get up in time?
- Do I disobey God in anything?
- Do I insist upon doing something about which my conscience is uneasy?
- Am I defeated in any part of my life—jealous, impure, critical, irritable, touchy or distrustful?
- How do I spend my spare time?
- Am I proud?
- Do I thank God that I am not as other people, like the Pharisee who despised the publican?
- Is there anybody whom I fear, dislike, disown, criticize, hold a resentment toward or disregard? If so, what am I doing about it?
- Do I grumble or complain constantly?
- Is Jesus real to me?

Now if you're a normal, full-blooded Christian, you won't need to go very far down the list before you're saying, 'God be merciful to me a sinner'! Of course, people will share at different levels but it's easy to make a start from such a list. At an agreed time—weekly, fortnightly or monthly—we meet together in threes for an hour, maximum, and use the questions as a basis for prayer. Each person will share a need from the list and invariably the other two will identify with it. We find that the secret of these sessions lies in a strong mixture of honesty and humour. I was in a cell recently where one man began to share at length about the state of his work, his wife and his children, then chipped in a word at the end that he was 'fine spiritually'. So I said, 'That's great, you've no problem reading your Bible then?'

'Oh, well actually, I haven't managed to read it for a couple of weeks.'

'And how's your prayer life?'

'Well, er—not too good.'

I then suggested that we might need to go back to question number one and read it out loud. That led to laughter, then honesty prevailed, reality set in and we helpfully tackled some important issues. As Bonhoeffer put it: 'When the morning mists of dreams vanish, then dawns the bright day of Christian fellowship.'[8] Cell-based churches don't have all the answers on being real with one another, but the emphasis on sharing truth and sharing weakness is awakening a fresh degree of honesty and accountability among its members.

'Come, follow me... and I will make you...'
(Matthew 4:19)

Now I'd hate you to think that being in a cell means being locked into an endless cycle of intense sharing and prayer ministry. The fact is that Jesus spent much of his time simply sharing his life with the disciples. They ate together, walked and talked and rested. They went fishing and climbed mountains, they visited the market place, the synagogue and the ordinary home. That's why cell-based churches shun the idea of a cell group merely being a meeting. If disciples are to be made and grown, then our lives need to be shared in a wider way. As a popular phrase puts it: 'Christianity is caught rather than taught.' When I think about all that I've learned as a Christian, I don't think about conferences, books or churches I've attended. Instead, I constantly recall the impact that various individuals have had on my development. I could probably list a huge host of people, but I know that five in particular have had a profound influence. As it happens, one or two of them are very well known, but they were neither more influential nor more highly valued than those who were much less known. Each one in their own unique way managed to touch and mould a part of my life.

When I was fourteen, a man called Donald Woods led me to faith. He was my chief in the Campaigners (a Christian uniformed organization), and I'd watched his amazing commitment with a bunch of unruly kids over three years. Week after week he'd turn out and run the evenings, and week after week we gave him a hard time, especially when it came to the boring epilogue! I can't remember Donald being a great communicator, but I do remember him breaking down one evening as he shared the gospel. That night I responded, and he continued to show me the meaning of compassion and vulnerability at a very vulnerable age. Meanwhile, from the age of ten, I'd had my feet under the vicar's table. His son was my best friend and I later married his daughter! Apart from being attracted to and intrigued by the bustle of a busy Christian home, I was far more impressed by the vicar's commitment to me as a mixed-up teenager. Whenever I had questions, he'd spend hours in his study with me explaining and encouraging. Cecil Butlin is remembered by literally scores of men and women whom he encouraged into full-time ministry. He had a gift for encouraging potential in the youngest Christian, and although he was a busy man, I learnt the value of availability from him.

I was privileged in my twenties to work with David Watson. I was then a full-time singer and worship leader, and used to lead his travelling team of Christian artists. Together we travelled the world, and that was my first full-blown exposure to Cell (though we didn't call it that at the time). Four days a week we met together to share and pray, and it was a baptism of fire for any unsuspecting, half-hearted disciple.

David expected much from his young and temperamental team, but he also modelled what he was asking for, and amazed us time and time again with his willingness to listen and learn from younger brothers and sisters. He taught me many things, but especially the value of accountability.

When I left David's team for theological college, I was grateful to have George Carey as my tutor. I'd met George a couple of years before at Greenbelt and had been struck by his approachability. That quality of cheerful and transparent openness steered me through a couple of theologically frustrating years. Nothing seemed to rattle George and nothing ever distracted him from simply being himself. He continued to convey all that in later years and never more so than when he was enthroned Archbishop. All over the cathedral were heads of state, monarchs, politicians and senior bishops. But surrounding him on Augustine's throne with the best view in the house were all his mates—his family, friends and a group of ex-students! George taught me the value of approachability in no uncertain terms.

And then last but not least came Harry Wilson, the vicar with whom I was a curate. All I remember of Harry is his grace and humility. When many of my colleagues seemed to be suffocating and discouraged in difficult parishes, Harry was an amazing enabler. Willing to take risks and let his assistant take the lead, he allowed me to run with one crazy venture after another and never once put me down. He simply believed the best of people and produced the best.

Now I don't need to tell you that all those men also had feet of clay. None of them was perfect and I learned from their weaknesses too! But anything I offer in ministry today has been shaped and inspired by their example. What was important in them all was not their words or the position they held but the sharing of their lives, watching them deal with life's issues, seeing them happy and sad, amused and irritated, relaxed and under pressure. I know that most of us won't happen to have a future archbishop as tutor or even a godly vicar as a father-in-law! But my experience of these men as mentors has led me to want to see a church where everyone can have the opportunity of open relationships with more mature Christians, a place where

nurture can happen naturally. Those of us who've had such opportunities can easily assume that it's the norm in Christian experience.
The fact is, however, that personal mentoring is a hit-and-miss affair
in the average church fellowship. If I'm fortunate enough to have
inspiring friendships, caring leadership or a good relationship with the
vicar, I might indeed feel that I've been mentored and encouraged
along the way. But if I'm just an average pew-filler, and if I can't get
close to the leaders, and if I clash with the vicar, then the options run
out very quickly. What's needed is a clearer network of relationships,
where each and every person has the opportunity for several levels of
friendship and support. The cell-based church provides this. From the
outset, every person is introduced not only to other cell members, but
a cell leader, assistant leader and cell sponsor. They also have constant
contact with their cell pastor and area pastor. They may not relate well
to them all, but there's quite a strong range of relationships and
support here, and every cell member has it.

It's interesting that since we moved to a cell-based model, we've had
far more times of testimony in the life of the church. I believe it's
significant that not only is there more to share and rejoice over, but
most of those testimonies pay tribute to one or more people in the cell
network who've helped, encouraged and influenced them. Indeed, the
norm now is for the cell leader, cell pastor or the group themselves, to
stand at the front with the person sharing, a very natural and often
moving symbol of the significance of friends and mentors.

'Put out into the deep water...'
(Luke 5:4)

We've talked about sharing lives, sharing truth and sharing weakness.
One other key strand in cell churches is the sharing of gifts and
experience. A word that is used consistently here is the word
'equipping'. Teaching should never be seen as a head-filling exercise
but as a heart-filling experience that equips people to serve. Jesus
constantly encouraged the disciples into deeper waters. Stretching

them into new ventures, he'd send them out and then, on their return, encourage them to reflect on all that had happened. The cell church does this in two ways. First, there is a systematic and ongoing training programme for leaders. Every few weeks they meet together to reflect on their experiences. Input is given by the teaching staff, but the emphasis is on learning from each other, sharing problems and committing them to prayer. At the same time, an equipping programme is put in place for the whole church. Beginning with the Alpha course, similar programmes are slowly built into the life of the cells, again with the emphasis on equipping. For instance, the Alpha awayday idea can be expanded to include Equipping Days and Encounter Weekends (as they are often called). Topics such as prayer, evangelism and spiritual warfare can be taught in depth.

One of our most exciting courses is taken from Rick Warren's 'Purpose-driven church' programme and is called 'Getting into SHAPE'.[9] The course is designed to help people discover the shape God has made them, and enable them to discover their ministry. It's more than a course about gifts and really aims to equip people. It covers *spiritual gifts*, where a person's *heart* and passion lies, what their natural *abilities* are, what kind of *personality* they have, and what *experiences* they bring. As people go through the course, they discover how and where they are best suited to serve, and end it with an interview to talk through the options. Most cell churches will have a series of these courses running through the year.

An important thing to remember, however, is that cell churches are constantly programme-pruning in order to focus more strategically on these courses and events. At St Mark's, we pruned down our Sunday services. Although our Sunday evening service was well attended, we discovered that for most people it was their second, optional service which they sometimes chose to attend. To make room for equipping, we closed down the service and began an evening event called 'On Track'. People are given three or four options for teaching and training, and now come in greater numbers. At the same time, we've discovered that many people simply can't come on a Sunday evening, so courses are often run as a 'one off' over several weeks on the main cell evening. The cell will come as a group and the evening will include group work so the sharing continues. Again and again the two main principles prevail: that cell is at the centre and the programme has to be pruned. In this way, a careful balance is maintained between teaching truth and sharing lives.

'Everyone who hears these words of mine and puts them into practice...'
(Matthew 7:24)

At the end of his sermon, Jesus immediately followed his 'Lord, Lord...' comment with the parable of the wise and foolish builders, and the need for strong foundations (Luke 6:46–49). It was a powerful picture because he talked of things that look very similar on the surface. Both men in the parable were trying to build something similar with the same materials, and both buildings were subject to the same storms. In fact there was probably no difference between them, apart from the foundations.

There's a dramatic illustration of that in York where thousands of people come each year to admire the Minster, one of the finest-looking cathedrals in the world. A few years ago, however, they discovered that York Minister was about to collapse because of very weak foundations, and they only just saved it in time and at considerable cost. In the same way, it's easy to build a church that looks impressive on the outside with a reputation for fine teaching and quality worship. But what's important in the end is whether disciples are being made, people who are slowly and steadily learning to do what Jesus says as well as proclaiming him as Lord. Any church can reproduce a Sermon on the Mount, but how many can consistently produce changed lives? The vision of cell is to take up that challenge and meet it head on.

Cell outline

Welcome

Think of one person who has had a major influence on your life. Share with the group how they influenced you.

Worship

Play quiet background music, and use Psalm 119 to centre your thoughts on the gift of God's word. Read out several verses at a time, for example verses 9–16, 17–24, 25–32 and so on. (It's a very long psalm, so be selective!) Pause several times, and respond to the psalm's message with short prayers of praise, confession, thanksgiving and petition.

Word

Read Luke 6:46–49.

- Share briefly who or what has helped you most in building your Christian foundations: sermons, books, conferences, leaders, friends, specific advice.
- Come prepared to share one thing that you feel God has been saying to you recently. It could be based on a recent sermon, a personal 'quiet time' spent studying the Bible and praying, a discussion or a book you've been reading. But where possible share a verse of scripture that reinforces and confirms it. As you share, try to be honest and real about your weaknesses and concentrate on encouraging and identifying with each other.

Witness

- Where people have shared a particular struggle or need, pray for them first.
- Returning again to the 'Witness' suggestions in Chapter 2, spend some time either planning your 'event' or praying for people on your *oikos* list.

Chapter 5

Value No 3: Creating Community

When he had finished washing their feet, he put on his clothes and returned to his place. 'Do you understand what I have done for you?' he asked them.

JOHN 13:12

Surely this had to be the most significant cell meeting in the church's history. It was the night before Jesus died, the final few hours before he was taken from his disciples. If ever the time was right for them to demonstrate all they'd learned, this was the moment. Before Jesus intervened, however, the moment almost descended into farce. Put aside the serene and clean linen image of Leonardo's Last Supper painting for a minute, and imagine what really happened. Remember this is first-century Jerusalem, where most of the roads and alleys were covered with a thick layer of dust, not to mention the droppings of various animals and other interesting remains. Add a little rain at times (or anything wet), and we're talking liquid mud. No wonder, then, that the host always provided a slave at the door of his home to wash the feet of the guests as they arrived and removed their sandals. They would then sit down for the meal—only they didn't sit at all. They reclined on the floor, leaning on one elbow, and there was no table to hide their feet under! Imagine, then, how the disciples had filed into the room and taken their places in a circle, totally ignoring the foot-washing because that was for slaves. Before a word had even been spoken, the whole room was reeking of proud hearts and dirty feet.

Before we dismiss the image and assure ourselves that that isn't how our churches are run, I want to suggest that it is. The fact is that every time the church comes together, however serene the atmosphere might appear on the surface, there's an underlying awareness that things are less than perfect. Beneath the veneer of hymns and 'How are you?' clichés, we're only too aware of all the proud hearts and dirty feet. We're often conscious of tensions, conflicts, mistakes and misunderstandings that litter the lives of our members but we simply don't talk about them, at least not in that context. After all, we are meant to be worshipping and focusing on Jesus. The fact is, however, that Jesus is a realist when it comes to relationships. Far from opting for the polite and religious cover-up, he lovingly and ruthlessly exposes hypocrisy. Instead of ignoring it, he addresses it head on and gets to the root of the matter: 'Unless I wash you, you have no part with me' (John 13:8).

Let's face it, if that had been our little get-together, we'd have preferred to paper over the cracks. In fact we'd have done anything to avoid embarrassment or conflict, especially on such an important night. The problem is that such avoidance leads to even greater hurts and complications in the long run. It's rather like the story of the little girl who was asked to say grace when the guests were invited to dinner. She turned to her father and said, 'But daddy, I don't know how to say it.' He replied, 'Just say what I said at breakfast this morning.' So she put her hands together and said, 'Oh God, those awful people are coming to dinner again today'! I told that story once and somebody came up afterwards and told me of a similar incident, only this time it was true. On that occasion the little girl got up during the meal and began stroking the back of the guest. When he asked her what she was doing, she replied, 'My daddy says you've got no backbone and I'm just checking'!

Now we cringe at stories like that, but the fact is that most of us are quite proficient at tying ourselves in knots in the complex world of relationships. At times we struggle in our dealings with other people and we react wrongly or badly or not at all. Whatever we do, though, it often comes back to haunt us when we don't deal with it cleanly and honestly. Meanwhile, the rest of the world is only too aware that life is essentially about relationships and the battle to get on with people. They recognize all too clearly that community is important, but all around them they see conflict and sadness. No wonder, then, that they demand a decent model from Christians before they'll believe. In a sense, we're talking about a shop window for the kingdom. If people like what they see through the glass, they'll enter the building. And if people like what they see in the Christian community, they'll begin to enter God's kingdom. But what if the shop doesn't produce what the window promised? Disillusionment can hit hard and the sobering truth is that too many new believers fail to settle and belong because they fail to see a loving church.

So what is a loving church? For a start it's not the kind of love portrayed in this little American rhyme:

> *Love is swell and so enticing,*
> *Orange jell and strawberry icing;*
> *Chocolate mousse and roasted goose.*
> *It's ham on rye, banana pie.*
> *Love's all good things without a question.*
> *In other words—it's indigestion!*

It's a silly rhyme, but it sums up the discomfort we can feel when love is simply expressed in sweet and sickly clichés and kept on a superficial level. Real love and genuine community begin only when we break through the thin veneer of our meetings and find practical ways of dealing with our dirty feet! Unfortunately, it's all too easy for small groups to do the opposite. As a young Christian student I can remember struggling in fellowship groups. Too often, discussions degenerated into the sharing of theological concepts or 'precious thoughts'. The sharing of burdens tended to mean sharing other people's problems instead of our own ('please pray for my friend'). When we did share it tended to be very superficial and we never dreamed of dropping our guard and talking about the deeper issues in our lives. In fact, I used to travel around Christian Unions giving concerts, and the favourite song of the day was a spoof on community life in CUs. Sung to the tune of 'You don't get me, I'm part of the union', it began with the words, 'You don't get me, I'm Christian Union', then:

> *Whenever you feel down, and if ever I'm around,*
> *You can come and see me and we'll have a cup of tea*
> *But only if you're sound!*

Alongside it I wrote a more serious song called 'Make it Real'.

> *We can hide behind our Bibles*
> *And pray aloud our prayers,*
> *Talk about our unity*
> *And the way we'll always care;*
> *Share about the good times,*
> *Show off all our zeal;*
> *But it's all just a waste of time*
> *If we never make it real.*

We certainly tried to be sincere in our Christian Unions and we meant well, but an emphasis on theological pride and individual piety kept everything very firmly on a superficial and non-relational level. The problem, of course, was that many of us had come from churches that actually encouraged this, so we really didn't know any better.

All that began to change when I moved to St Michael-le-Belfry in York. As I lived and worked with David Watson's team, we'd meet regularly with a rigorous agenda for real sharing, and two things were gently discouraged. We learned on the one hand that it wasn't helpful simply to share a Bible verse and its meaning without trying to say how God was speaking to us through it. And secondly, we were always encouraged to approach the sharing of pain in the same way. The team meeting was never to become a dustbin for dumping our problems, but rather a place of healing where others could help us discern what God might be wanting to do in our lives.

Of course there were days when we all needed space, and there were occasions when we all tried to cop out. Even David would have his standard scriptures and pat answers at hand when he wanted to avoid the discomfort of sharing. But he also modelled a more vulnerable path and generously taught us never to allow him off the hook! Much of this is described and explained in his own writings. He spoke movingly on many occasions of his struggle with depression and self-doubt. What isn't so well documented are the many occasions when he would be paralysed by it just hours before he preached and ministered to thousands. Many times we would gather around him in prayer as we wrestled together with our weakness. And many times we'd battle through our conflicts before teaching on reconciliation.

Behind the scenes and beyond all our gifts there was a powerful foundation of strong relationships, often born out of pain and forged out of conflict, but visibly and tangibly the basis on which the ministry was built. Over the five years that I worked with his team I came to appreciate the powerful effects of genuine and honest community. The Christian artists who worked on the teams were often professionally gifted, but in the end it wasn't those gifts that were noticed. Instead, again and again, people would comment on our togetherness and unity and servant attitude. We knew these came out of some very tough training, but we also knew that they were a hundred times more valuable than any of our artistic gifts.

Since then I've longed to see the church in general, and small groups in particular, get far more serious about community. To do that we need values and structures that encourage us on board and keep us on track. We need tools and opportunities to lead each other gently towards closer and more honest relationships. And as we do that we have to be ruthlessly honest about the cost. In the last chapter I began to suggest some of the ways that can happen. Indeed it's impossible to talk about discipleship without talking about community. We grow up as we grow together. But let's consider some more tools that enable that to happen, apply them to cell-based communities and reflect on the potential of cells in creating genuine community. The New

Testament gives a long list of practical instructions when it talks about relationships, and many of them come in the form of 'one another' verses. As I list a few of them here, you may want to consider how effectively you're able to apply them in your fellowship.

Be devoted to one another in brotherly love
ROMANS 12:10

'Brotherly love' is all about commitment. The word 'brothers' appears over two hundred times in the New Testament and it literally means 'from the same womb'. It reminds us that as Christians we're not just friends or followers of the same cause, but we're actually blood related in the spiritual realm. Bought by the blood of Christ, we become part of a family with all its conditions and commitments as well as its blessings. Of course, every family has its tensions and its ups and downs, the days when you fall out and the habits that drive you up the wall. But deep down there's a unique and binding commitment that we call 'covenant love'—the opposite of what we might call 'cupboard love'. Covenant love is based on commitment, not on feelings, and it's that foundation that makes it work: 'For better, for worse, for richer for poorer, in sickness and in health…'. When families go wrong it's often because they allow their feelings to override their commitment. Covenant love turns to cupboard love when people only do what they feel like doing, and that causes havoc in many marriages today.

It's exactly the same in the church. When Christians have no understanding of covenant love and commitment, they simply do what they feel like in the fellowship. They'll come to worship and home groups and ministry groups if and when they want to, and meanwhile, the rest of the fellowship can feel increasingly discouraged and let down and even devalued. Community will never be built on cupboard love. The church needs a foundational structure that will clearly model the importance of covenant. Cell provides that model. It sends a clear and positive message to every believer that they don't belong in isolation. They aren't just a set of individuals who take out a kind of club membership and then choose the services and programmes they will attend and the people they'll befriend. Instead, they're grafted into a small family unit that becomes their main spiritual home. Unlike the Sunday service, if they miss the cell they're really missed. If they contribute to cell, they're really appreciated, and when the cell reaches out and touches their lives they're really blessed. In fact, that's what makes the difference between a church with cells and a cell church. A church with cells has small groups as a part of its overall programme. A cell church on the other hand allows the cell to be the central, fundamental and essential tool for building church itself—a community built on love.

Staying with this verse from Romans for a moment, I particularly like the way it stresses that feelings are crucial too. It begins with the phrase 'be devoted', or 'show loving affection', 'love tenderly', 'love warmly'. This is the only time this word 'devoted' appears in the New Testament, but it's tied very strongly to another word that appears throughout the Bible and that's the word 'compassion'. Compassion in scripture means being moved to the very depth of one's being. It's used in the context of feeling deeply the needs and pains of another person. The Latin word from which we get our English word compassion means 'suffering with someone'. The Bible shows that when God wants to work with compassion, and to reveal it through his people, they always have to go through an element of suffering in one form or another. Hosea, for instance, uses the word many times. In his life and his writings, he brings a tremendous note of tenderness to our notion of God's love and its passionate nature. And yet Hosea himself went through the pain of a broken marriage and it was through that pain that he learned about the compassion of God for an adulterous people. In the New Testament, Paul is able to speak with tenderness and understanding because of all that he's been through. On many occasions he speaks of his pain and what it's taught him: 'Praise be to the God and Father of our Lord Jesus Christ, the Father of compassion and the God of all comfort, who comforts us in all our troubles, so that we can comfort those in any trouble with the comfort we ourselves have received from God. For just as the sufferings of Christ flow over into our lives, so also through Christ our comfort overflows' (2 Corinthians 1:3–5).

We had a text on our wall at home. It said, 'All I want is to know Christ and the power of his resurrection.' Around that time we were visited by a dear friend who'd gone through the very deep pain of losing his first-born son. When he saw the text he smiled and said teasingly, 'What about the rest of the verse?' The full text comes from Philippians 3:10 which says, 'I want to know Christ and the power of his resurrection and the fellowship of sharing in his sufferings, becoming like him in his death.' We don't have the text on our wall any more! This friend was being very perceptive. The fact is that we all want the power of his resurrection, we can't get enough of it. The danger comes when we emphasize the triumph and the joy and forget about all the hassle and suffering. But it's not an optional extra!

We all have to deal with suffering at different times, often in the context of relationships. But do we deal with it openly, with the help of others, or do we dive into our emotional bunkers to shut out the pain? C.S. Lewis once said that God 'whispers to us in our pleasures, speaks to us in our conscience, but shouts in our pains'.[10] In other words, he's never more close and never more instructive than when we're hurting. But the issue is whether we'll listen and learn, and that's where community is crucial. Time and time again I've valued the wisdom and encouragement of others, but never more so than when I'm hurting. It's then that we need encouragement to calm us, wisdom to guide us and discernment to protect us, and we don't always have it within ourselves. Being in community is an essential part of allowing God's love to touch us. Being in a cell provides a consistent, tangible and practical way of enabling that to happen.

Of course, there is another side to this. What happens when the pain is coming from the community itself, or when the cell is the source of suffering? How many times have we seen a group disintegrate through the pain of disagreement and division? In a cell-based church the covenant rule comes into play. If there's division we deal with it, and if it's difficult we try and learn to live with it. How does a beautiful pearl come into being? It appears in the first place because an oyster has to put up with an irritating object like a grain of sand. It has to cover that object with layer upon layer of smooth mother-of-pearl secreted from its own body. Do you have an irritating object in your life? (Think of his or her name!) All of us are tempted to imagine that the solution lies in getting rid of the object (or person). Often, however, God takes the sandpaper of our relationships and deliberately tells us to layer on his love and forgiveness. Eventually something far more valuable and attractive emerges, both in our lives and theirs. This part of our calling is a tough commitment but it's what brings resurrection, and it's what gives cells integrity and power. Division and disunity may never occur, but when they do there's a network of support and an agreed set of values that will always be applied.

> **Be kind and compassionate to one another, forgiving each other, just as in Christ God forgave you**
> EPHESIANS 4:32

Here's a verse that shows us how unity is worked out in practice. There are three simple directives here, all of them very practical.

Look for the good. The phrase 'be kind' translates 'think kindly', and that's where kindness always has to begin. It starts as we try and look for the good in people and believe the best instead of always fearing the worst. This phrase was a very powerful one for the early Christians. The word for 'kind' is *chrestos*, and the word for 'Christ' is *Christos*, so whenever a person thought or talked about being kind they'd immediately be reminded of Christ. 'Be kind' and 'be Christ-like' sounded very similiar. Now the Christ-like principle is that in every person you meet there is both good and bad. In all your relationships you can choose whether to concentrate on the good in people, and 'think kindly', or to focus on the bad. To use an example, a few months ago I decided to introduce a ministry-based cell for some of our singers and musicians. I led it myself for a while, not least because I was feeling frustrated by the up-and-down commitment of a few. The cell programme ensured that people shared what was really going on in their lives. They talked at different times of terrible tensions at work, frustrations at home and worries in the worship, and I very quickly felt ashamed of the superficial assumptions and judgments I'd made. The cell agenda itself enabled and encouraged me to think more kindly before I questioned people's commitment. It also led me to the second principle.

Learn to be vulnerable. Once again, mind and heart are balanced together because thinking well of people leads on to feeling and acting with compassion. The word 'compassion' or 'tender-hearted' here means literally to 'feel a person's heartbeat'. In other words we need to get in touch with people's feelings and respond from the heart. The cell group encourages that because it has a strong agenda beyond the meeting itself. Each member gradually recognizes that they have a responsibility to care for one another outside the meeting and to keep in touch. They also keep up to date with every pastoral issue because they continue to meet and share together every week.

Live at peace. 'Forgiving one another' is something we all need to become experts on, applying it with ruthless regularity. The fact is that none of us can avoid the forgiveness issue in a sinful world. We have to forgive and be forgiven; and yet the problem of unforgiveness is often rife in the church as well as the world. That in itself suggests that we need the help of others in resolving conflicts. We may need encouragement to go and *do* it and we may need others to be peace-makers as we go through the process. And we need at times to do it collectively as a group when division threatens. My experience as a pastor tells me that practical help and training in this area are essential in creating community. It also tells me that occasional sermons and pastoral counselling are not enough. There needs to be an atmosphere of grace in this whole area that lingers over the life of the church, and that can happen through cells.

Six principles are essential in resolving conflict and all six can be nurtured within the life of a cell. First, we need to resolve it *quickly*.

The unforgiving servant in Jesus' parable (Matthew 18) effectively locked himself in a prison, and that's exactly what we do when we don't forgive. We build mental lists of all the times we've been hurt until we are crippled and incarcerated. When Jesus said, 'Forgive and you shall be forgiven,' he was literally saying, 'Release, and you shall be released.' As we release people from the prison of our unforgiveness we ourselves are released. That's why we're told to do it before the sun goes down, as quickly as possible (Ephesians 4:26). Somebody once said that one of the secrets of a long and fruitful life is to forgive everybody everything every night before you go to bed.

The second principle in resolving conflict is to do it *quietly*. Keep the conflict between you and the person or people concerned and refuse to let it spread. We then need to do it *kindly*. Think about how you react and the way you communicate, and learn to express your feelings in a Christ-like manner. We may have feelings of anger, pain and frustration, but we can still express them in a way that's not going to make the conflict go nuclear. We need to do it *constructively*. Think about what this conflict is really about and let it be known that you want to resolve it and learn from it. Then do it *completely*. Don't play around on the surface if the conflict is a deeper one. Make sure you try and get to the real issues, because the conflict will keep recurring unless you do. That means that we need to listen very carefully to what the other party is saying. We may have grasped 90 per cent of the problem, but if we don't resolve the other 10 per cent the issue will return to haunt us. And then finally, we need to resolve our conflicts *continuously*. Be prepared to apply these principles again and again and to keep short accounts with people.

In the book of Proverbs we read that 'reckless words pierce like a sword, but the tongue of the wise brings healing' (Proverbs 12:18). The way of peace in our relationships depends heavily on the way we communicate with one another. Cell groups assist communication in three vital ways. First, they provide a training environment where we regularly learn to relate, communicate and learn from each other. Secondly, they provide a challenging environment where the state of our relationships will be regularly questioned. And thirdly, they provide an accountable environment where there's always a leader or friend or the group itself to help. Without that process, community remains an elusive dream. Let's look at a few more 'one another' verses that encourage our communication.

Encourage one another daily
HEBREWS 3:13

Spur one another on towards love and good deeds
HEBREWS 10:24

Confess your sins to each other and pray for each other so that you may be healed
JAMES 5:16

The emphasis in all these verses is on helping each other in the struggle against weakness and sin. They all seem to take for granted that we can't win the battle without mutual help. Whenever we sin, it has three consequences: it deceives us, paralyses us and hurts us, and all these verses suggest that the remedy lies not so much in more prayer but in more relationship.

When the writer of Hebrews says, 'Encourage one another daily,' it is so that 'none of you may be hardened by sin's deceitfulness' (v. 13). Left to our own thoughts and devices we soon begin to harden our hearts and deceive ourselves. But if we regularly surround ourselves with the support of others, encouraging us to do the right thing, it's harder to take the wrong route. When they also spur us on, the paralysis of the defeat we often feel is itself defeated. I believe that's also why we're encouraged to confess our sins to one another as well as to God. A single sin might easily be sorted with simple prayer, but when we sin continuously (as we all do!), it has a tendency to wound us. As well as feeling condemned and defeated, we are left with consequences that need to be handled and healed. The community that commits itself to sharing lives as well as meetings can provide that healing. I believe that's why our additional covenant cells are so popular.

Carry each other's burdens

GALATIANS 6:2

You may be thinking by this stage that cell life can suffocate people and take away their independence. Undoubtedly the call to community is a call to be more dependent, but a cell's agenda will always be to remind its members of their individual responsibility. It's interesting that immediately after Paul says, 'Carry each other's burdens' (v. 2), he almost seems to contradict himself by saying, 'For each one should carry his own load' (v. 5). The first word he uses means a very heavy weight, a burden that is too heavy for a man to bear alone. Undoubtedly cells are quick to identify these and are well equipped to respond. But the second word that Paul uses refers to a soldier's pack, which he has to carry himself. That is a burden which we have to carry and which we cannot and need not share, because it's light enough for us to carry ourselves. That burden is our responsibility to God for our own Christian growth. A cell group will never lose sight of that as it applies the word of God in practical ways. A heavy burden may be shared, but the gentle pressure of personal challenge is always there. Cell members are encouraged to support the weak, but never to make them weak by living their lives for them.

Accept one another

ROMANS 15:7

Submit to one another

EPHESIANS 5:21

Bear with each other

COLOSSIANS 3:13

Perhaps the greatest personal challenge in relationships is to love the people we don't naturally like and commit ourselves to being alongside them. Our natural tendency is to say, 'Love your neighbour as yourself—just choose your neighbourhood!' It can really cause chaos when our small groups turn into cliques and people shop around until they find a like-minded group. If they can't find one, they opt out. When the small group itself becomes the heart, soul and focus of the whole church's life, however, there's a very strong encouragement to belong, become involved and to believe it can work. We don't naturally bear with, accept and submit to people we neither know nor understand. But as we get to know their needs and struggles and see where they're coming from, it's much easier. It's also an essential lesson if our worship is ever to take off. The full passage in Ephesians 5 reads like this in the original: 'Speak to one another with psalms, hymns and spiritual songs. Sing and make music in your heart to the Lord, always giving thanks to God the Father for everything, in the name of our Lord Jesus Christ, *submitting* to one another out of reverence for Christ' (vv. 19–21). In other words, submitting here is very much in the context of our worship together.

Any genuine Christian community will include a variety of people at different ages and stages, and with different tastes, preferences and prejudices. The challenge of community is to blend them all together. We have to foster an atmosphere of tolerance and submission where, for example, people learn to appreciate the songs and hymns they don't like for the sake of their brothers and sisters who do. As cell groups learn to worship, pray and talk together, they get experience of each other's preferences, and learn what it means to be more accepting and tolerant.

Let's not end this chapter, however, without recognizing that the way of acceptance and tolerance is a difficult and sometimes messy road to travel. We may, for instance, encourage each other to be real, honest and courageous in our sharing, only to find that some in the group react insensitively or, worse still, fail to keep matters confidential. It goes without saying that these issues need to be constantly and consistently addressed in practical teaching, but the greater stress needs to be laid on the fact that people do fail and will make mistakes. The church is not a haven for the super-holy but rather a hospital for sinners who are still being healed. Michael Harper, a leader and writer in the whole area of spiritual renewal, wrote:

To accept community means to lay down your life. It involves taking risks— without antiseptics. True love is always vulnerable. It can be hurt easily. Community is never easy. It means to allow yourself to be known as you really are, and to let the inevitable abrasive situations turn you into a new person.[11]

Serve one another in love

GALATIANS 5:13

As Jesus took a towel and washed Peter's feet, Peter dug a deeper and deeper hole for himself: 'You shall never wash my feet... Not just my feet but my hands and my head as well! ... I will lay down my life for you.'

'Will you really?' said Jesus, and predicted his denial (John 13:6–9, 37–38).

Left to ourselves, we fail every time. We blame, deny, exaggerate and make excuses till we're backed in a corner with nowhere to go. Jesus showed us how to serve in so many ways, but it's the towel of truth that he uses first as he creates community—speaking the truth in love. After his denial, Peter probably just wanted the ground itself to swallow him, but by the time he stood and preached at Pentecost he was probably profoundly thankful for the foot-washing episode. Cell life can be costly, but it can also lead to a Pentecost.

Cell outline

Welcome

How do you let off steam when you're feeling angry or irritated with someone?

Worship

Write out all the 'one another' verses from this chapter on to slips of paper.

Either:

1. Play some music and quietly pass the slips of paper round the room. As you receive a verse, respond to it silently in worship, asking God what he's saying to you through it, then pass on the verse to another person and read the next one as it's passed to you.

Or:

2. Invite each person to choose a verse and to lead the group in a prayer based on its message.

Word

Read John 13:1–17.

- Imagine you are the disciples, writing a letter to Jesus a few weeks after Pentecost. What would you want to say to him now about the way you had handled the night before he died? What would you want to say about how you had learned and changed in your relationships?
- Looking through the list of 'one another' verses, which in particular would you feel that God was wanting you to work on at the moment?

Witness

Where you feel able, share about any particular relationships that you find difficult at the moment, and that affect your witness. Pray very specifically for one another in this area, and agree to support and encourage one another in seeing a change in these relationships over the coming weeks.

Chapter 6

Value No 4: Doing Evangelism

Just then his disciples returned and were surprised to find him talking with a woman. But no one asked, 'What do you want?' or 'Why are you talking with her?'

JOHN 4:27

I guess this was another tough day in the disciples' training school. Starting early with a long, hot journey, by midday they'd have been ready for a break and a bite of lunch. They'd also be feeling very uncomfortable as they made their way through Samaria. Four hundred years of enmity between Jews and Samaritans wasn't exactly going to evaporate as Jesus passed through, and they knew it. Nevertheless, they were learning to be servants so, as Jesus rested, they walked the extra mile and went looking for food. Having found it, they retreated out of the town and away from potential trouble and returned for a well-earned rest. They expected a quiet lunch, but instead they found Jesus quietly setting off an earthquake!

It says they were 'surprised to find him talking with a woman' (v. 27), which is a very moderate translation. The Greek text literally says that they were 'astonished', 'bewildered', 'in a state of amazement'. In fact they were completely mind-blown for three reasons. First, he shouldn't have been talking to a woman in the first place. The rabbis said that it was forbidden to talk to a woman on the street, let alone have an intelligent conversation with her: 'Better that the words of the law should be burned than delivered to women'![12] In addition, this woman was a Samaritan, and Jews and Samaritans had never been on speaking terms. To add insult to injury, this woman had a reputation that would give any man seen with her the image of a kerb crawler.

Jesus couldn't have made the disciples feel more embarrassed or uncomfortable, and John hints at that when he says, 'But no one asked...'. What could you ask in that situation? 'Have you completely lost your mind?' Once again, however, Jesus was planning that they should lose a few things like prejudice, fear, indifference, complacency, pride and lack of faith.

What's significant for me in this episode is that Jesus 'had to go through Samaria' (v. 4). It was not the kind of place a Jew would choose to go through and most would have made the effort to take a very long detour. But he had to do it. He had an inner compulsion telling him that in kingdom terms it was the right and the only thing to do. Not only did Samaria need the gospel, but it lay there in his immediate path as a direct challenge. I want to try and address that challenge in this chapter because we all face our Samarias. Samaria is the place where we feel uncomfortable, challenged, stressed out, embarrassed or simply not at home. It's the feeling we have at work when we know that we're the only Christian there. It's the tension we have with our friends when our values clash on important issues. It's the feeling of frustration and pain when we don't even feel at home with the family we love because of our beliefs. It's the place that we know we have to pass through on countless occasions, and it's a place that has left many of us feeling defeated when it comes to evangelism. We've heard the sermons, learned the principles and received the message, but Samaria is an alien and hostile place that we'd rather avoid. I expect the disciples felt the same way. They were on a very steep learning curve at this point but they were also learning fast. A few months before they may have refused even to enter Samaria and certainly wouldn't have shopped for food there. Their experience of cell life was definitely changing hearts and building confidence and the discussion after this episode would probably have been fascinating, to say the least! But what was it that might have spurred them on and what is it that cell groups can provide in encouraging our witness? As we look at this, I also want to illustrate how each of the five cell values interrelate, and how impossible it is to isolate one from another. Each of them is vital in building a cell-based church and all of them are relevant in doing evangelism.

All involved

Christian writer Dr James Kennedy made an interesting calculation about evangelism. He imagined a famous and gifted evangelist, able to draw thousands every night to a packed stadium. Meetings were held every evening of every week, and 1000 people came to faith at each meeting, but even so he worked out that it would take ten thousand years for the whole world to come to faith (and that was ignoring the population explosion).

He then imagined every Christian winning one other person for Christ every year, and training that person to be a disciple who would also win one other person every year. Again he did the sums and discovered that it would take only 32 years for the whole world to be converted!

Jesus sent out his disciples two by two for mission (Luke 10:1). In doing so, he didn't set apart the gifted preachers and build a support team around them. Instead, he saw the potential in every single person to be a dynamic missionary agent. But he also never dreamed of leaving the individual to do it on his own—they were all involved together. Cell-based churches take the 'two by two' principle very seriously, but it looks very different from the two-by-two door-knocking that is sometimes envisaged. From the beginning there's a commitment to do evangelism and to overcoming the fear of it. But there's also a healthy recognition of the Samaria syndrome and the need to overcome it. Cell groups take account of the very real difficulties and take time to address them. Every week at least half an hour is set aside to focus on our witness. Every cell member has an up-to-date list of the people they live and work with, and those people are prayed for regularly inside the cell. They may focus on just one or two in a meeting, but the very act of bringing these people before God in the context of the group has an uplifting and faith-building effect.

In addition, the cell is committed to making friends and building bridges, working alongside each other to make disciples. One way or another, everyone in the cell becomes increasingly involved in each other's Samarias, easing the pressures, lightening the loads and offering constant encouragement.

The focus of each cell's witness will be different. Although we all have colleagues, neighbours, family and friends, cells will tend to concentrate on different areas at different times. It's interesting that when we first embarked on a cell strategy at St Mark's, none of the cells had a particularly distinctive character. They were simply brought together from the existing membership. Three years later, however, many of the cells have a membership that reflects where their heart has been in terms of witness. One cell has been filled with members of the same family, half of whom have come to faith through the deliberate witness of the cell. Two groups are now heavily flavoured by members of the police force! The cell focused on the workplace and has drawn in colleagues one by one. That cell has since multiplied and the original cell leader is now the cell pastor. Other groups have become neighbourhood cells as they've built bridges within a particular street or locality. Some have become interest-based as they've shared a similar hobby, and others are linked by a similar experience (such as bereavement). Some are age-group-based, like our twenty-something cell that has recently run its own Alpha course in the local pub. Others have become ministry-based as they've focused on a role inside the church. In this case, musicians or children's leaders will meet together, and the intention in their witness is to draw people on the fringe into deeper discipleship by getting involved in the ministry. People who've attended the services but never entered into the whole life of the church are themselves prayed for and encouraged into the life of the cells. Similarly, there are cells which specifically reach out to those who have drifted away from the church altogether. Each and every group is encouraged to be specific and intentional in its witness, never trying to take on too much, but always aiming to be focused and fruitful. Increasingly the cells are like a tapestry of different colours and shapes, all sharing the same values, but each distinctive in its own right and focusing on its own witness. How, then, does all that involvement develop?

Becoming disciples

The emphasis in the second cell value is on the word 'becoming'. Discipleship is a process that never ends and the story we share is never of a single event but of a journey with many landmarks along the way. Effective cell groups identify those landmarks, especially the ones that are instrumental in leading us to faith. Let me identify four of them and describe how cell groups will concentrate their witness in these areas. Again (as for the five cell values) I've arranged them in alphabetical order:

- **A**sk and intercede
- **B**reak out and bless
- **C**ome and see
- **D**ecide and receive

The first two remind us of God's invitation to us, and the other two of the invitation we offer to others.

Ask and intercede

Before we do anything else we need to look at our hearts and our attitude to non-believers. One of the most profound lessons I've learned about prayer is the effect it can have on our hearts, especially in the realm of relationships. I remember as a young Christian receiving some very practical teaching on loving your enemies. I was struggling with a particular relationship and someone drew my attention to the verse that says, 'Love your enemies and pray for those who persecute you, that you may be sons of your Father in heaven' (Matthew 5:44–45).

The principle is that when we talk to God about people and tell him our feelings, he shares his own heart with us. The more we spend time with the Father in prayer for a person, the more we begin to see them as he sees them. Gradually his vision of them rubs off on us until we eventually become a 'chip off the old block', responding to them as children of our Father in heaven. I believe that's an invaluable principle in praying for non-believers. A passion for evangelism is never something we can manufacture or systematically learn. It's something that comes out of the heart once the heart has been changed. That's why we have to be serious about prayer before we can even think about witnessing.

When we do think about it, however, we often find that it's the first obstacle we meet on the road to evangelism. We know that prayer is important but we also know how poor we are at it and how easily we falter. But when we agree to do it together on a regular basis with a proper strategy, things begin to change. Cell groups are encouraged to be active in prayer in specific and strategic ways. Reading the New Testament, you'll find that Paul, for instance, never prayed for God to save people. He knew that it is God's desire to save and that people are free to decide, so what you find is an emphasis on praying in two particular areas—both of which contribute in making the gospel freely and powerfully accessible to people. First of all, he placed an enormous emphasis on praying for an outpouring of God's Spirit on the church. For the Ephesians, for instance, he prayed for wisdom, revelation, knowledge and enlightenment (Ephesians 1:1–19). For the Colossians he prayed for the knowledge of his will and for 'a life worthy of the Lord', 'bearing fruit in every good work', 'strengthened with all power' and for 'great endurance and patience' (Colossians 1:9–11). For the Philippians he asked for an abounding love and depth of insight, discernment, purity, blamelessness and righteousness (Philippians 1:9–11). In other words, he prayed for their equipping and for the quality of their witness. He also prayed for boldness in preaching, acceptance of it, safety in travel and rescue from danger.

In short, we're to pray for anything and everything that will allow and equip the church to communicate the good news freely and powerfully. As we do that, however, we recognize a few obstacles that need removing and that's where the other emphasis lies. In particular, we're encouraged to resist the devil (James 4:7) and remove the mountains (Matthew 17:20), conscious that 'the god of this age has blinded the minds of unbelievers, so that they cannot see the light of the gospel of the glory of Christ' (2 Corinthians 4:4). This means that as we pray for our network of unchurched friends, we're to concentrate on being specific and strategic. Of course we'll pray for their physical needs and for blessing in general. But when we start praying for their spiritual needs we begin by resisting the enemy and his influence over people, and then we ask God to remove the obstacles that are keeping them from receiving the message. We then pray for an outpouring of God's Spirit on that part of the church that is going to communicate God's love to them and look for the results. I believe that's how it should work in practice, carving out time to pray together in this way, and doing it faithfully, week by week, both in our cells and individually, encouraging and involving all.

Break out and bless

Several years ago we had a vision to break out of our church building. Like many churches, we had an increasing burden to be relevant to the outside world and to build some bridges. For us it meant some radical reordering. We closed the building for nearly twelve months and literally knocked down the walls. We knew that we had life on the inside but from the outside we looked like an empty, shut-down church. Wedding and funeral parties would often congregate outside the forbidding doors, then huddle through our tiny porch into a rather cold and austere environment that was obviously alien to the unchurched stranger. The fact is that an old church building, steeped in history and full of personal memories, may feel like a comforting friend to the average faithful member, but to the person who rarely comes and doesn't understand its rituals, it can present a very different and decidedly unwelcome image.

As a result of the work, the building itself was transformed, but the internal reordering that went on inside the life and heart of the fellowship was far more significant. Being out of the building and inside the local school and our church hall brought the obvious reminder that the body of Christ is made up of people rather than bricks. But it also reminded us that the gulf between the world and the church is wider than ever and needs many more bridges. The more we wrestled with our aims and vision, the more we came to see that it's one thing to open the doors of our building to occasional visitors, but quite another to start opening windows of understanding, acceptance and friendship to those who don't share our faith. Increasingly we began to examine our motives and ask ourselves some challenging and painful questions. Were we really wanting to welcome people or simply build an attractive worship centre? Did we really want to serve God in the community or just have a platform from which to preach our faith? Were we really willing to meet people where they were and make them feel at home, or were we only building a spiritual home for ourselves?

In one of his wilder moments, our architect had sketched out a design that made our building look like a futuristic supermarket. Every wall was made of glass and every panel was a doorway. The principle was to create as many entry points as possible and to eliminate every obstacle. In the end we settled for something more modest—but we embraced the principle with passion. When we reopened, we began to think of ways in which our new building could bless the community and make them feel at home. We developed a restaurant in our new church extension called 'The King's Table' and provided home-cooked food throughout the week. We put on supper events and started a catering service out in the parish. We even provided take-aways for teachers at the local school and buffets for the local health centre. We also encouraged special interest groups and hobby groups. A craft group called 'New Creations' attracted one kind of person, while the newly formed golf society swiftly grew to 60 members, two-thirds of whom were unchurched. More recently, we have launched an exciting street project called 'Action for Kids'. One of our young men felt increasingly burdened by the numbers of young children on the streets at all hours. Many of them were bored, unsupervised and often at risk. He started to watch and walk the streets, making friends with the children and clearing away the needles dropped by drug users. Then he began to organize events, befriend the parents and build up a team to help him. That in turn has led to another bridge between church and local community as a ministry to the underprivileged families has developed. This now provides food and clothing, debt counselling, and practical help on parenting issues.

In all these cases, the ministries have evolved out of two growing convictions. The first is the call to become good news before we present and proclaim it. The second is the need to build bridges for that to happen. Our church has been on a learning curve for some time in the realm of evangelism. Like many churches, a few years ago we rediscovered the fact that evangelism is a process rather than a one-off event. We then began to recognize the importance of relationships and friendships in the process. Finally, we've been rediscovering that friendship with non-believers is about loving and being a blessing with no strings attached. That may seem very obvious, but this particular lesson can be an elusive one for the church that believes in the priority of proclamation. The sad fact is that churches can be so busy teaching truth and proclaiming good news that they forget to live the truth and be the good news. When we do choose to try and touch people's lives, we tend to focus on the people we like and live with and understand already. Of course, in every church there are good and bad examples of Christian witness, but the challenge is to create a whole new culture in the life and fabric of the fellowship itself. What is needed is a witness like DNA code, imprinted on every church member, and that's where the cell comes into its own. Written into its agenda, the cell group learns to grapple with the challenge to break out and bless. They aim first of all to build up friendships within their *oikos* network and invite the cell to get involved. A neighbour, for instance, may be struggling with a very practical problem. The cell may be able to provide the expertise and help. Someone else's widowed mother may be about to move house. Again the cell can move in and provide manpower. Problems are solved and friendships are formed as Christians share their resources.

Come and see

Gandhi is reputed to have said, 'I might have become a Christian if I could see one.' The fact is that if people want to see Jesus today, they have to see him through his body, the Church. Telling the story of Jesus is, of course, paramount to evangelism, but the story of his body gives it an additional ring of integrity and truth. At the same time, not many of us are blessed with the gift of teaching and relatively few can explain the complexities of our faith. Everyone has a story worth telling, though, and that's a basic tool in the guide to witnessing. All of us can be well armed and ready equipped with our own little testimony. All it takes is a question and the story can be told. What gives it additional power, however, is the story of our church, particularly if it's in the present tense. A delightful offshoot in our own reordering project was a dramatic increase in the number of witnesses. Suddenly, our shyest members were enthusing about their lovely new building and telling the story! Invitations to 'come and see' were far more attractive than the challenge to 'come and hear' as word spread through the community. Since then the subtle shift from hearing to seeing has continued and increased. 'Would you like to see our restaurant?' 'Would you like to see what we're offering our children?' 'Would you like to see what's been turning my life around?'

It's what I call the 'Antioch principle'. One of the first great Gentile cities to see an explosion of Christian growth was the city of Antioch (Acts 11:19–30). When you read the story, the emphasis is not on great leaders but on a great crowd of nameless witnesses, the *laos* as they were called, the 'little people' who spread the message in countless conversations. That's what happens when the church has a story. It doesn't need to be dramatic but simply attractive enough to say 'come and see'. Cell-based churches will provide the 'come and see' event as part of their programme, but the cell group itself provides the real attraction. Anything from a social evening to a cell guest night can provide a showcase for the cell with a story to tell (see Appendix 3).

Decide and receive

Current material on evangelism often refers to three stages in a person's journey to faith—believing, belonging and behaving. They rightly argue that we hinder the process of evangelism when we convey to people that they need to believe and behave differently before they can belong. A generation that now feels alienated by church needs to be drawn into a place where they can belong, and then begin to learn what it means to believe and behave. During the last decade, the Alpha course has demonstrated that superbly. Its emphasis on friendship, food and welcome has provided an ideal environment for people to explore the faith and make their way in slowly. Cell-based churches reinforce that thinking by focusing on longer-term strategy. Relationships take time to develop and we don't earn the right to speak in a matter of days. Even a ten-week course will sell a person short if we're sincerely wanting to model a new way of living. That isn't to say that people can't be touched by God directly and believe independently, but for those with a barrier to God and a grudge against the church, belonging may come first by a very long mile.

The moment comes, however, when decisions are made and grace is received, and we need to be sensitive to the culture we live in. That culture now tells us that we live in a post-modern world, a pick-and-mix society where belief and behaviour are a matter of personal taste and preference. The emphasis now is not simply on decisions about right and wrong and truth. The truth in the end is what is right and wrong for you, and that may well mean embracing a little of this belief and a bit of the other. No longer can we assume that a decision to follow Christ is a decision to embrace all his teaching. The nurturing process has always been important for the new believer, but it's now paramount if the church is to survive.

What, then, does nurturing mean? What it doesn't mean is simply taking someone through a faith and doctrine programme. Once again, it's about living together in relationship. Let me use an example. Like all parents, I've tried through the years to give quality time to my children. I've blocked off the diary and organized trips and events and various treats. But when I look back, the most significant times have been when I've simply been 'hanging out' with them. In fact the most intimate moments have come during a taxi ride (me driving!), or a game of football or waiting in a queue. Those are the moments when questions are asked, struggles are shared and hurts can be healed. They couldn't be scheduled in a diary but just have to happen when the time is right. Like all families we still have a battle to find those moments, but we have learned that it's about values and lifestyle and not about programmes and calendars. And that, in essence, is what cell life is all about. The Alpha programmes and equipping courses are very important, but accountable and loving relationships are crucial in working and wrestling through what it means to be Christian. In cell churches, the receiving process is emphasized far more than the moment of decision, and the person who nurtures becomes more significant than the one who preaches. Belief and behaviour change as truth is modelled inside the community.

Creating community

On a recent visit to Asia I was not only impressed by the staggering rate of the church's growth there, I was also moved by the amazing sense of community and commitment to one another. In fact, the simplest sociological study of Far Eastern culture tells us that the group always comes first. Not only is loyalty to the family a top priority, but there's a sense across the whole of society that the group exists to support and help each other, and that people rise and fall together as a whole. A study of western culture, however, shows the opposite. In the west, we emphasize the value, dignity and rights of the individual. No wonder, then, that churches across China and South East Asia are not only exploding, but almost entirely cell-based! The same would be true in South America and parts of Africa. Bearing this in mind, Bishop Festo Kivengere once described evangelism as 'the overspill of fellowship'. The apostle John did the same when he wrote: 'No one has ever seen God; but if we love each other, God lives in us and his love is made complete in us' (1 John 4:12).

If God reveals himself through community and community life is poor, then the church in the West needs to be very practical in working at its weaknesses. At St Mark's, we soon realized that doing the four Ws was not suddenly going to change our natural habits when it came to community. We recognized that our lives were too crowded and the church was too busy, and many of us were not even developing our Christian friendships, never mind our witness to non-believers. We needed down-to-earth decisions to help us practise what we believed, so we came back to the two fundamental principles of pruning and allowing cell to be central (see Chapter 2). Prayer and community are two of the essentials in 'doing evangelism' and we weren't doing either in any depth. We decided to carve out more time in the cells themselves and released one meeting in four for those two things. Every fourth week, the cells now alternate between having either a social evening or a night of prayer. To make it easier, we brainstormed a list of ideas and passed them round the cells, then got started (see Appendices 3 and 4). Every month now the whole church is either chilling out together (and inviting others to join them), or reaching out in creative prayer. Either way, they focus on evangelism and emphasize the 'doing'.

Look at the fields!

Back in Samaria, the disciples' eyes were opened. There they were with their eyes on the well and all they could see was a loose woman and a very alien place. But John then gives us a beautiful picture as the crowds swarm out of the town and through the fields towards them. The image is powerful and moving as Jesus turns them around and says, 'Open your eyes and look at the fields! They are ripe for harvest'. (John 4:35). A few moments of relational evangelism and the whole town had come alive to the presence of God. As Peter rubbed his eyes and received a little more truth, I wonder if he thought back to his own conversion. Luke tells us that as Jesus was teaching the crowds at Gennesaret, Simon Peter wasn't exactly hanging on his every word. He was busy washing his nets. Jesus grabbed his attention when he 'got into one of the boats... and asked him to put out a little from the shore' (Luke 5:3). By the time he'd put out into deep water and given him a record catch, Peter was convinced and transfixed! They 'pulled their boats up on shore, left everything and followed him' (5:11). To do evangelism, very simply, is to get into people's boats. It means moving out and climbing in with them, standing where they stand, doing what they do and helping them do it. For a while it can feel as alien as Samaria, but then Samaria was transformed as the people encountered Jesus. Let's look, then, at the fifth value that completes the picture of a growing cell.

Cell outline

Welcome

Name a place or event where you had to go but didn't want to (either as an adult or a child). What happened and how did you feel?

Worship

Read Revelation 21:1–7.

Play an appropriate piece of calm, instrumental music and imagine a window into heaven. Ask yourselves the following questions (invite someone to read them out, with pauses in between):

- What do you see, hear, smell and feel?
- What do you notice about its beauty, laughter, joy, healing, love?
- How is it like our own world?
- How is it different from our world?
- What are people doing?
- Imagine suddenly seeing Jesus. What is he doing?
- How would you respond if you were standing there now?

Thank God for what you see in your imagination. Pray that he will give us a taste of heaven in our walk with him. Pray especially that others may catch a glimpse of heaven as we love and live with them.

Word

Read John 4:27–42.

Sometimes God confronts us with uncomfortable challenges in witnessing. What would be an uncomfortable challenge for you in your witness? Is God speaking to you about it through this story?

Discuss together the four stages mentioned in the chapter:

- Ask and intercede
- Break out and bless

- Come and see
- Decide and receive

In which areas would you say you were strongest and weakest at the moment? In what ways do you feel (as a church and as a small group) you might be able to build on your strengths? Which particular weak area could you address as a priority?

Witness

Identify any areas where you can 'look at the fields' and see them ready for harvest. Pray about what you see: for example, friends who are open to the gospel at the moment, clear and obvious opportunities in the neighbourhood, workplace, home, and so on.

Value No 5: Encountering God

Then they came to Jericho. As Jesus and his disciples, together with a large crowd, were leaving the city, a blind man, Bartimaeus (that is, the Son of Timaeus), was sitting by the roadside begging. When he heard that it was Jesus of Nazareth, he began to shout, 'Jesus, Son of David, have mercy on me!' Many rebuked him and told him to be quiet, but he shouted all the more.

Mark 10:46–48

If ever anybody was ready for an encounter with Jesus, it was Bartimaeus. Everybody else was on their very best behaviour as the Great Physician passed by—all except Bartimaeus, who started yelling at him. He didn't care what people thought of him as he grabbed hold of his chance to be healed.

I've always loved this story, but what always used to puzzle me was why the Lord asked such a seemingly foolish question. Here's a blind beggar, trapped in a life of poverty and despair and he's screaming for mercy. Jesus responds to him by saying, 'What do you want me to do for you?' It was obvious! But on another occasion, in John 5, he asked a similar question of a man who'd been crippled for 38 years, lying beside a pool just waiting for someone to help him into the water. Jesus came up to him and asked, 'Do you want to get well?' (v. 6). If it wasn't Jesus asking the question, you'd probably think he was mocking the man. Of course he wanted to be well! He'd probably spent the last 38 years thinking of nothing else. But let's have a closer look at the question. Literally translated, it reads, 'Do you *really* want to get well?' And to Bartimaeus, 'What do you *really* want?' In other words, he was probing them, and he needed to do so. The crippled man had probably got very accustomed to being carried around. He'd never had to work or take responsibility for his own life. In fact, when Jesus asked him the question, he didn't give him a straight answer. Instead he started telling him all about his sickness and his awful life.

What do you really want?

If we're honest, there's something in us all that enjoys the perks and security that sickness often brings. I used to love being sick as a child. It was great to stay off school for a while, but it was all the attention and sympathy I really enjoyed, especially when they extended to chocolates, comics and all-day television! Seriously, though, it is possible to have this terrible tension in our lives. On the one hand, we can be really suffering with physical, mental or spiritual sickness, and long to be healed. On the other hand, we can secretly cling to our sickness because it doesn't make demands of us in other ways. Jesus knew that and wanted to test these men. Did they really want everything that Jesus was offering, or did they have their own agendas that needed addressing first?

Whenever a cell group meets, the same question is asked and it comes across loud and clear. Do you really want Jesus to be present? Then always allow time for worship before you give time to the word. Do you really want to hear what God might be saying to you? Then ask questions that apply your Bible study in practical and personal ways. Do you really want to take the Great Commission seriously and obey the call to go? Then make sure that you focus specifically on that before you leave the cell. It's very clear from the other four values that cell groups set out to avoid playing religious games. We're here to be honest, real and practical and that means that we need more than just a pleasant spiritual experience. What we need is an encounter with God that changes our perspective then changes our lives. To find all that, we need a change in our expectations.

What do you expect?

Somebody once offered this additional beatitude: 'Blessed are those who expect nothing, for they shall not be disappointed.' The truth is that years of disappointment in struggling churches can either lead to no expectations or the wrong ones. The disciples were never disappointed once by Jesus, and yet after three years they still weren't expecting all that Jesus promised. What they needed was a supernatural encounter and the book of Acts begins on that note:

And when they came together, he gave them this order; 'Do not leave Jerusalem, but wait for the gift I told you about, the gift my Father promised. John baptized with water, but in a few days you will be baptized with the Holy Spirit.' When the apostles met together with Jesus, they asked him, 'Lord, will you at this time give the Kingdom back to Israel?' Jesus said to them, 'The times and occasions are set by my Father's own authority, and it is not for you to know when they will be. But when the Holy Spirit comes upon you, you will be filled with power, and you will be witnesses for me in Jerusalem, in all Judea and Samaria, and to the ends of the earth.' After saying this, he was taken up to heaven as they watched him, and a cloud hid him from their sight. (Acts 1:4–9, GNB).

The last crucial words of Jesus focused on expectations. Once again they'd got it wrong when they asked: 'Are you at this time going to restore the kingdom to Israel?' They were busy thinking about politics and the outward signs of power and Jesus made them focus on the inner power of the Holy Spirit. In the same way, it's crucial that you and I don't get so caught up with strategies and the outward signs of being church that we lose sight of the real and only source of spiritual power.

A few years ago my wife and I were having a short break in a friend's beach house. During the stay, we decided to take the owner's little outboard motor boat and sail up the coast. Our expectations were high as we filled the boat with food, towels and other gear and pushed it into the sea. I then started pulling the cord on the motor, and nothing happened. Half an hour later, we'd drifted out to sea without any power. I was tugging, my wife was rowing, the two of us were arguing, and the heavens opened. It was then that I spotted a little red switch at the back of the motor. One little flick and the fuel was released and the boat came to life! I've never forgotten that day, not least because the tale itself is a rather good parable for the church. We can have all the resources and tools at our disposal and yet still end up rowing along in our own strength. Many of us will continue to be disappointed and exhausted in ministry until we rediscover where the power lies and how to release it.

Spiritual power

When they saw him, they worshipped him; but some doubted.
MATTHEW 28:17

The first thing we should recognize about the power that Jesus offers is that it *overlooks our weakness*. Looking at Jesus' cell group after three years, you might be forgiven for dubbing it 'the cell from hell'! He's poured his life into them and taught them meticulously and yet it says in Matthew's account that even now 'some doubted'. Of course recent events in Jerusalem would have left them reeling and confused. But even those who believed in his power didn't really understand the nature of it. As Jesus prepared to leave them, he could have been forgiven for being extremely discouraged. Far from that, he confidently predicted that everything was about to change, as indeed it did (Acts 1:4–8). First, however, their whole vision needed changing to enable them to see what Jesus had in store. That began to happen as they returned to Jerusalem and 'all joined together constantly in prayer' (v. 14). No doubt they reflected on three amazing years and shared story after story of the blessing they'd seen. By the time the Day of Pentecost arrived, they were still 'all together in one place' (2:1) and they were ready for receiving something special.

As I've watched cell groups developing over the last three years, I believe something special has happened to our church's confidence.

As they've 'joined together constantly' with an agenda for sharing, the cell experience has been changing their expectations and expelling a few doubts. Many factors are responsible but one has had a particular impact. The whole approach to cell meetings ensures that testimonies are shared on a very regular basis and are seen as a major priority. Someone shares a need and the cell prays. The need may be personal, practical or spiritual, or it may concern someone or something outside the group. Whatever the need, the cell receives ongoing feedback until they see some practical answers to prayer. The point is that sharing is not a one-off event with a single 'help them, bless them' type prayer. Instead, the cell walks alongside from week to week in an accountable way until situations are seen to change. When they do change, the mood of the group changes too. Some groups even keep a prayer diary and systematically log each and every answered prayer. As cell members are encouraged to develop in ministry their confidence grows further and again the testimonies multiply. As time passes, the volume and variety of testimonies increase until there's an atmosphere of expectation around the whole church. Not only are testimonies shared within the cell, but the most encouraging ones are brought into the Sunday worship and shared from the front. To coin a phrase, an 'attitude of gratitude' increases people's vision till they begin to see that God surrounds us with his blessing.

All this reminds me of a true story of a group of sailors who were marooned on a life-raft off the coast of Brazil. After days without water they were on the verge of death, but a passing ship eventually rescued them. When the captain of the ship asked them why they were so dehydrated, they replied that they'd run out of water. 'No water?' said the captain. 'You only had to reach over the side of the boat for an endless supply'. They'd been floating through a freshwater stream that pushes out into the Atlantic from the Amazon River. The shortage was an illusion. All they had to do was drink. Many churches have the same problem. If the fellowship is struggling, it can feel as if it's floating and dying in a barren environment. What we need is a new focus that enables us always to be on the lookout for fresh blessing, so that when it comes, we start shouting and sharing it from the rooftops. All of us need the constant reminder that God's power is available now and that it's there for the weak. The shortage is an illusion—we simply need to drink.

'You will be baptized with the Holy Spirit.'
ACTS 1:5

The second thing that Jesus teaches about his power is that it's meant in the end to *overwhelm our lives*. As an Anglican I might be tempted to think of 'baptism' as a gentle sprinkling with a few drops of water. Perhaps that is also what comes to mind when we think of the Holy Spirit's touch—a few drops, gently sprinkled. But the word 'baptize' here means literally to overwhelm, to plunge, to drench and saturate. When you read through the rest of the book of Acts, you begin to accept what an appropriate description it is of the disciples' experience. It also goes well alongside the word he uses for power—*dunamis*—from which we get the word 'dynamite'. In other words, when we talk about encountering God, our expectations should be very high.

Why, then, is that not a common experience in many churches? I'm thinking here of Christians who welcome the teaching in this area, but often feel that they won't receive a 'drenching' of blessing outside the occasional big event or special experience. I believe we have a clue here in this word 'baptism'. Imagine a sponge as it gets immersed in a bucket of water. The sponge itself is filled with water and when you take it out of the bucket, the water continues to pour out of the sponge. In a way that's a very good picture of the way our personal blessing is supposed to overflow into those we meet. The more we are filled with the Holy Spirit, the more we overflow and become effective witnesses. Of course, that can only happen if the sponge is fully immersed in the first place.

But let me take the picture a stage further. Whenever I decide to wash my car (which isn't very often!), I usually find that the sponge has grown very hard as it's collected dust in the garage. When a hardened sponge is immersed, it doesn't absorb the water at first. It usually becomes wet on the outside, but it needs a little more time to soften in the water before it can be filled. As Christians, a week in the real world can begin to harden us around the edges. It's not that we've become cynical or stopped praying, but the pressure of life can dry us out very quickly. What we need, not only in our quiet times alone with God but in our life together, is a multitude of opportunities to soak in the presence of God. I use the word 'multitude' because God moves in a multitude of ways, and he uses different methods in different moments to touch different people. He also offers a perfect balance when it comes to the ingredients of blessing. It's not simply a case of receiving more truth or more spiritual experiences. We need a strong blend of both. As somebody put it, 'All word and no Spirit, we dry up. All Spirit and no word, we blow up. Spirit and word together, we grow up.'

Even before we embarked on cell church principles, St Mark's had begun to develop a 'soaking' culture. Being an Anglican church with a strong blend of tastes and traditions, we soon realized, for example, that one man's meat is another man's poison when it comes to prayer ministry. Any church can develop in one particular way and draw its congregation from a particular group of people. The challenge of a parish church is to welcome and appeal to the whole community, and the whole community is a mish-mash when it comes to personality and tastes! We therefore tried to create a whole variety of ministry opportunities that would appeal in different ways to different people. Apart from modern and traditional services, prayer ministry was offered both during and after the services. One week the opportunity came in the context of communion. Another week it came with an appeal after the sermon.

Keeping our ear to the ground, we discovered that other people who wanted prayer weren't coming. For some, it was the fear of walking to the front. For others it was the fear of never knowing who might pray with them. For a significant number, it was the fear of coming a second time and appearing greedy! Little by little we provided more opportunities for people to come. We spoke about the importance of coming continuously and seeing healing as a process. We also began ministering in people's homes in a more strategic way. When serious illness or pastoral issues arose, we would offer to come as a team to pray with people at home. The team would consist of a couple of leaders and the person's own choice of friends and family. We worshipped together and then prayed, and once people had experienced this in a safe environment, they began to take hold of the other opportunities too. Nowadays, there are queues of people at every service, all coming with the healthy expectation of a deeper encounter with God. They know that it may or may not include a sudden dramatic healing, but their main confidence lies in God desiring to bless them in this context as much as any other.

Cell churches value quantity, quality and variety when it comes to encountering God. The emphasis is not simply on a desire to be filled, but on the simple fact that we all 'leak' continuously and need regular opportunities to refill. When the American evangelist D.L. Moody was once asked why he never stopped talking about the filling of the Holy Spirit, he replied, 'Because I never stop leaking!' In the average cell group, there's a fundamental acceptance of this. Apart from the opportunities I've mentioned, the cell group itself learns to value the need for soaking. That's why the worship time is never rushed, and why praying for one another takes a high priority. If an icebreaker uncovers a need, the cell addresses that need—if necessary at the expense of a whole evening's programme. Slowly but surely, each and every member learns to become involved in praying for others. Each group learns at a different rate and ministers in different ways, but the desire for spiritual power and the key value of quality encounter with God is pursued by all.

'The gift my Father promised, which you have heard me speak about...'
ACTS 1:4

The problem with talking about power is that it can carry connotations of being out of control and out on the edge when it comes to ministry. Certainly Jesus' words here pose a challenge to relinquish human control and take a few risks in being church, but the power that he talks about is the kind that *overcomes our fears*. He speaks about it here as the gift 'which you have heard me speak about' (Acts 1:4), and the last time he taught about it he talked of sending them 'another helper' (John 14:16, GNB). In the New Testament there are two words that translate 'another'. One of them means 'another of a different kind', but the word that Jesus uses means 'another of exactly the same kind'. In other words, when Jesus spoke about the Holy Spirit, he explained that everything he had been to them the Holy Spirit would be too. All the love and gentleness, grace and compassion that they had experienced in him would be exactly what they would experience through the power of his Spirit. It's a power, then, that for all its intensity is overflowing with the love of God and simply overcomes our fears.

I learnt that lesson on a personal level as a young Christian student. Around that time, there was a lot of unhelpful debate about second baptisms and some very polarizing views on the work of the Holy Spirit. I attended a house-party that was tackling the theme, and on the Saturday evening there was an invitation to be filled with the Holy Spirit. I was extremely nervous about it, but joined a group of others who gathered together to receive prayer. We sat around a log fire and the leaders made their way slowly around the semi-circle, ministering to each person. All of us were invited to offer our own prayer first, and the whole process took about an hour. We had come from various churches and traditions and what touched me deeply was the way in which each person had a totally different and very personal encounter. For some it was a fairly dramatic affair and for others it was a quiet and dignified embrace. In every case, the Holy Spirit met people where they were, and touched them at their own point of need. There was no hype, no control, no expectations other than a personal and powerful encounter. For my own part, I needed peace and a little less fear and I received it in full measure. So powerful was the sense of God's love and gentle grace that I completely let go of every anxiety and argument I'd been wrestling with. Getting my head around it all was still important, but the Spirit gave me the one gift I needed above anything else at that moment. Since then I've had many encounters at many different levels, but I've never lost sight of the fact that the Spirit of Jesus takes us just as we are, and works with power at the level we can handle.

One of the major attractions of a cell-based ministry is that it meets people where they are. We've seen already that cell groups are challenging places to be and certainly not the most comfortable form of fellowship. But there's a very comforting emphasis on accepting people as they are and allowing them to grow one step at a time. Without that emphasis it would be impossible to welcome and integrate new people. Cell church is equally uncomfortable with chandelier swingers, precious thinkers and boring Bible bashers. The aim is to be a community of supernaturally natural people who connect with the real world and keep their own personalities intact. What that means in practice is an incredible variety of cells at very different stages with many different flavours. That in itself is exciting, especially as they still manage to share the same values, follow the same programme and worship in the same church. God cares passionately about unity and delights in diversity, and cell churches aim to celebrate that.

Let me try and illustrate all this with the story of one particular cell in the realm of prayer. For a group full of relatively new believers, the idea of encountering God in prayer for a whole evening can be extremely daunting. Here's how one cell began to handle it.

When we were a house group, prayer didn't feature high on our agenda. Bible study and discussion, yes! But when it came to prayer it would be a short closing prayer at the end of our session, usually prayed by our leader. The new cell format challenged us about our lack of prayer and our attitudes to it. Becoming a cell meant giving serious thought and space to this whole area of praying! Because we had so many fears and inhibitions when it came to praying out loud we decided to spend one of our cell evenings looking at 'why' we need to pray and at 'how' we might be encouraged to do it! We began by sharing our fears, breaking into the silence, worrying about saying the 'right' words, not being sure what to pray for and thinking others were better at it than we were. We read Hebrews 10:19–25 together and realized that our confidence in coming to prayer is entirely through Jesus, no merit or worth of our own. God wants us to meet with him and has provided the way.

We sat quietly and relaxed while soft background music played and we imagined ourselves sitting opposite God himself. He smiled, pleased that we had come. We thought back over the day, something good, some little thing that we had enjoyed and quietly in our hearts we thanked God. Was there anything unpleasant, an irritation, words spoken which we wished we'd said differently? We told God about it, in the silence. We brought to mind someone we love whom we long to be in a deeper relationship with God and we named them in our hearts. Lastly we thought about something in the news recently that affected us, maybe made us feel angry or sad, troubled or fearful. We told God about it and how it made us feel. Then we were asked to think about just one thing we had prayed quietly in our hearts and to share a one-sentence prayer out loud. Each person prayed a simple prayer and for some of us that was the very first time!

That prayer evening was a turning point and since then we have found other ways of encouraging each other and slowly growing together in praying out loud. One such way is a prayer basket, where we each write a short prayer on a piece of paper, fold it up and put it into the basket. When it's time to pray, we each take one and read it out in turn. It really helps to be speaking other people's prayers and we've been amazed at how much 'in tune' our prayers have been. Another time we were given a large pebble or stone to hold. We closed our eyes and imagined the weight of the stone to be a burden we wanted to give to God, a worry, a problem, a sin. One by one we placed the stones down, giving our burden to God and leaving it there. No words were spoken out loud, but afterwards we shared how God had blessed us.

One more thing that is special to us is when we stand together holding hands in a circle and pray a very simple prayer for the person on our right/left. We have been so encouraged in seeing one another grow into prayer and to be able to share our feelings, joys and concerns in a safe and loving environment. We find that the things we focus on as we pray together in our cell carry over into our own personal prayer times. Cell is helping us to become more disciplined in our 'quiet times'. We still have a lot to learn and experience but we do thank God for his patience and his love and for the way that he has enabled us to grow and develop without feeling pressured or threatened. (See Appendix 4.)

'You will receive power when the Holy Spirit comes on you; and you will be my witnesses...'

ACTS 1:8

Perhaps the most authentic hallmark of the Spirit's power is the way in which it *overflows to others*. 'You will receive power,' says Jesus, and then 'you will be my witnesses'. He doesn't talk here about wanting them or commanding them to be witnesses. He's saying if you are authentically filled with the power of God, it will turn you into a witness with a desire to make Christ known.

Using another water picture, if I'm holding a glass full of water and you bump into me, what spills out? Answer: whatever's inside the glass. And when you and I bump into people as we go about our business, what spills out? Answer: whatever's inside the heart. If our hearts are angry, bitter, envious or sad, that eventually overflows. But if our hearts have been filled with the love of Christ, then that will also spill out. And we won't need to grit our teeth and see it as our solemn moral duty to witness! It's interesting that whenever any of our cells are solemn and saying it doesn't work, it's usually because the worship and witness aren't working. A cell may be very effective in studying the word and praying for each other, but if its encounter with God isn't real, the witness won't happen. Similarly, if it squeezes out and waters down the witness section, it quickly feels discouraged and dry. That's why Paul wrote to Philemon 'I pray that you may be active in sharing your faith, so that you will have a full understanding of every good thing we have in Christ' (v. 6). Full understanding comes only as we fully embrace all the values of our faith.

'Do not leave Jerusalem, but wait...'

ACTS 1:4

When we begin to take this gift of power on board, it should do one other thing. It should *overturn our complacency*. There's only one clear command in this passage and that's the instruction to wait. However, it's not the word we use for sitting around waiting. Rather, it's the word that's used in the sense of waiting on tables, actively working and serving. The word reminds me of my administrative assistant. Each week, she produces a list of jobs that I need to attend to—letters, articles, rotas and references. She then sits back for a day and waits. But often the work isn't forthcoming (because I haven't got my act together!). Then she gives up waiting for it and starts to wait upon me, saying, 'You haven't given me that letter—I need it today—I've been waiting for days—do you want me to pick it up?' Some might call it pestering and nagging, but it's wonderfully effective over a period of time! It's that kind of waiting that Jesus requires of us in receiving his power. Love by its very nature will never force itself on us, and God will always wait until we wait upon him with the very clear message that we want all that he's giving. I don't know about you but I've often had to repent of my weakness in this whole area. It's so much easier to 'wait for' than to 'wait upon'. What I need is the discipline of a time and a place to do it and the encouragement of a cell to do it with. Cell churches supply the incentive and the resources to do it.

Sitting by the roadside, Bartimaeus had got used to waiting, but he had a real flair for the other kind. By the time Jesus stopped and asked him what he really wanted, he didn't need to think about it. In fact, the story ends on a wonderful note. Jesus healed him, gave him his sight and gave him a free hand. He said; 'Go… your faith has healed you' (Mark 10:52). Which way, then, would he go? He'd been sitting on the Jericho road for years and years, and Jericho was the big sin city of the day. He'd probably heard all those people coming down the road talking about what a cool and exciting place it was. He may have been thinking that that's where he'd head if he could ever see enough to enjoy himself. But as soon as he was healed he followed Jesus (v. 52), and Jesus was heading in the opposite direction, to Jerusalem. Cell churches will always lead us back to Jericho and Samaria for our witness, but first they will focus our eyes on Jesus and Jerusalem. They will take us to the cross and on to resurrection and then lead us to the encounter of Pentecost. Only then will we be ready for Jericho again.

Cell outline

Welcome

Think of something that you wanted badly enough to make some sacrifices for. What was it and how did you get it?

Worship

Read Mark 10:46–52.

Begin with a time of silence, reflecting on the question, 'What do you want me to do for you?' Apply the question to yourself, your group and your church. Ask yourself what obstacles you may need to remove and throw aside in order to receive from God. After a time of quiet, pray together and express what God has put on your heart. Guard against praying selfish prayers. Reflect instead on the choice that Bartimaeus made and try to focus on the quality of your own discipleship.

Word

What are your expectations in encountering God? What would you like to see more of in your experience as a group?

God's power:
- overlooks our weakness
- overwhelms our lives
- overcomes our fears
- overflows to others
- overturns our complacency

Which of these points do you feel particularly challenged or encouraged by? How might you respond as a group?

Witness

To what extent does the life of your group overflow to others who are on the outside of the group? Have you arranged an event yet to enable that to happen? If so, are you encouraged? If not, what are the difficulties in arranging this? Share your experience so far and ask God to teach you more in this area.

Chapter 8

Celling the Vision

Jesus said to the servants, 'Fill the jars with water'; so they filled them to the brim. Then he told them, 'Now draw some out and take it to the master of the banquet.' They did so, and the master of the banquet tasted the water that had been turned into wine.

JOHN 2:7–9

It wasn't all trials and challenge in Jesus' company. The wedding at Cana gives us a wonderful flavour of life on the inside. Wouldn't you have loved to see the master of the banquet's face as he tasted the wine? Often it must have been amazing, exciting and fun to see the kingdom of God in action. Jesus never just left people talking about his teaching. He invited them to 'taste and see'. A few years ago I was preaching on that very theme in Sweden, and invited people to come and talk to me after the service. A beautiful blonde girl appeared and attempted to say, 'I would very much like to talk to you.' What she actually said in very broken English was, 'I would very much like to taste you'! Apart from making me go weak at the knees, it reminded me of the radical difference between talking and tasting. There's really no comparison, and the challenge of any vision is to take us beyond all the talking and teaching and on to the tasting. How can we help our church (and ourselves) to taste and see this vision for cell church? And what will it take to make the transition?

Pursuing the vision

I've learned four things about vision as a Christian leader. I want to mention them here because they permeate these last two chapters.

First of all I've learned that any vision God gives to his church will be *a challenging vision*. Read about any vision in the Bible and look at the impact on the person who receives it. In every case, people are stretched and challenged to move beyond where they are at the moment. Moreover, it's impossible to follow any vision of God without experiencing a few growing pains. It's healthy and it's to be expected.

The second thing we can expect is *a changing vision*. The God who says, 'Do not dwell on the past' (Isaiah 43:18) is the God of the new song, the new heart, the new spirit, new mercies, new name, new covenant, a new creation, and a new heaven and earth. He remains the same but his people need constant renewal, so a recurring theme in scripture is, 'See, I am doing a new thing!' (Isaiah 43:19). Just as the early church moved into one new phase after another as they followed the Spirit, we must do the same. Before any church can embrace a God-given vision, it must develop a culture of change where the 'new thing' is expected and welcomed.

When it is welcomed, we'll also see that it's *a unique vision* that will go on changing. God loves variety and diversity, so we should never try and clone the church. Too often we see a good thing and are tempted to create replicas that we then fossilize for all time. God's way is to give us the same DNA, with the same values and principles, but with a unique identity on the outside. The more I look at cell churches, the more personality I see in each and every one.

I believe God also wants to give his church at the local level *a shared vision*. Jesus had a passion for unity and majored on it in the discipling process. He modelled it, commanded it and died for it, yet we often allow our vision to split the church! If the process of imparting vision divides a church, it doesn't necessarily mean the vision is wrong, but it may indicate that it is too soon, or that the process of imparting it has not been sufficiently well planned. So let's look at a process for selling the vision of cell church.

Preparing the ground

If there's only one thing you draw out of this book, I hope it's the importance of values. Before any church changes its structures, it's vital to check out the values. If we 'do what we value and value what we do', then it's important to begin by asking what we value most in the church at the moment. How much value do we place on each of the areas described in the last five chapters? How is that reflected in what we're now doing? It's not enough to say 'that sounds good'. Our vision and values need to begin to look good before we even contemplate a transformation of the structures.

Some time ago, we discovered at St Mark's that our structure was not the primary issue that needed addressing. In fact, dealing with structure is a push-over compared to the problem of attitude. One person summed it up when they wrote out what they felt God was trying to say to us:

Come to me afresh now, and bend. Lay your life before me. Lay it down. For how can I bless if you stand rigid, upright, proud, uncompromising, arrogant? I long to bless you and my church, but butter will only spread if it is soft. If it is hard and cold it tears the bread, and those who stand rigid and arrogant tear my body. Agape love spreads and flows. Melt in the warmth of my covenant love, so that my love can spread out through you and cover many more people. Be pliable in my hands and in humbleness and repentance allow me to spread my love, my power, my glory on to so many others.

Even those who were not entirely happy with words of prophecy like this could see the importance of what was shared. Like many others, our church grew from a root of bitterness and division. Nearly 100 years ago it broke away from the mother church and the parish was literally divided in two. The PCC minutes over the next 80 years at times read rather like a version of the history of English warfare! Hardness and unforgiveness often prevailed and it sometimes showed in the worship. I remember watching the music group inviting the congregation to stand. Half immediately rose to their feet and sang while the other half folded their arms and scowled.

A year later, our motto verse was 'Let us love one another', and I began to apply a principle that I'd learned from John Wimber and Juan Carlos Ortiz. They both used to talk of preaching and teaching on a single theme for a whole year until the message had soaked in and been received. I wasn't courageous enough to face a whole year, but we did spend four months from Christmas to Easter on the theme of attitudes and relationships. In every service, at every meeting and every home group, we made our way through all the 'one another' verses, all the fruits of the Spirit, and all the passages on Christian fellowship. As Easter approached, the whole atmosphere began to change. People were beginning to value the importance of right attitudes and relationships in a new way. Since then we've revisited the whole area. The last time, we did a four-month series called 'Watch Your Mouth'. That may seem a little intense, but we all saw the funny side of feeling that the whole congregation had seen the power of hurtful words and were walking around with invisible plasters over their mouths! We still have a very long way to go, but anyone who now comes to the church is in no doubt that this is a fellowship that places value on right relationships. We continue to fail, but there's an overwhelming sense that we value seriously how we treat each other.

What is important is looking at values before we think about vision and strategy. If people don't really value the need to grow up in Christ, grow together in love and grow out in witness, then the introduction of cell church will be a disaster. That's why we need to involve every member in the process. A leader may embrace the values and teach them consistently, but to what extent has the church as a whole received them? I hope that talking through the contents of this book will be a helpful tool in that process. We need to be ruthlessly honest about where we believe we are now, and at what pace we believe we can move forward. It's essential to recognize that there's no such thing as an instant cell church. I've been fortunate enough to have had over a decade to work through these values within the same fellowship. But some may be starting from scratch. The important thing is not to rush, but to go a step at a time and never stop moving. A wise friend of mine used to say that most people overestimate what can be done in one year, and underestimate what can be achieved in five years. I've found that to be a remarkably accurate account of the way in which things have progressed at St Mark's. So have a passion for progress, but have patience along the way.

Planning the transition

There are two main routes to becoming a cell-based church. The first is to follow a 'prototype' approach, where a group of leaders start with a single cell. Their aim is to model the vision, weed out the problems and learn from their mistakes. Once the cell is working as it should, it begins to multiply and then other members of the church are gradually grafted in to an authentic healthy cell church.

The second approach is called the 'big bang'. Here the whole church is prepared at the same time, the existing home groups are closed and the transition is made together. Both approaches have their strengths and weaknesses. Most cell church textbooks put the case for prototype and are well documented. I have taken the 'big bang' route and it's working for me! Let me highlight three main issues in looking at the two routes and address them from a pastoral perspective.

Quality

It's argued that it's almost impossible to put a whole church into transition at once because chunks of the congregation will not immediately be able to grasp hold of the whole vision. The major question facing traditional house groups is 'can a leopard change its spots?' Will the church continually revert to its traditional form and never really transform into a true cell model? A comparison is often made with industrial prototypes, where the product is refined, tweaked and tested until it's ready for general distribution. The problem is, however, that we're not dealing with a product here but with fallible and sensitive people, and there's no guarantee that the prototype will ever be ready on time (look at the disciples!).

When I was considering the options, I was in contact with two friends who were running with the prototype approach. In both cases, after one year the cell had disintegrated along with the vision. Soon after, St Mark's began its transition with 33 cells. Knowing my congregation, I basically argued that we had 33 chances of getting it right! Seriously, I knew that some of the groups would flounder, but I expected others to surprise us all. I also knew that the best prototype was not necessarily going to come from the existing leaders. By its very nature, cell has a wonderful way of drawing out hidden potential and releasing a natural pool of model cell members. Three years on, and we have a mixture of healthy cells and failed cells, but the strong and the weak are working in harness. Because a cell-based church is strong on accountability and quality control, this means that the whole church is working together to encourage the weak. Indeed, I don't know of a church anywhere in the world that doesn't have struggling cells, but I do know that cell church values have a way of releasing grace and renewal wherever there is weakness.

Unity

As a local church pastor, I've worked for many years at building bridges, promoting unity and healing division. My instinct, therefore, is to take the whole church forward together and not in small slices. The problem with gathering and promoting a particular type of group is that it runs the risk of sending out the wrong message about being the body of Christ. The charismatic movement had to learn the lesson when it used to talk freely about first and second baptisms. The danger with prototype cells is that they can gradually create the feeling of a first- and second-class church, however well they are presented.

Integrity

At the end of the day, the most attractive thing about cell church is its focus on values. At the heart of those values is a deep desire for genuine community and effective evangelism. If cells are going to model community, how far can they do that if they operate on a separate track to the rest of the fellowship? And if evangelism is going to concentrate on the unchurched, will it not cloud the vision and weaken the focus if prototype cells are busy mainly drawing in the existing membership?

Let me say here that I believe both 'prototype' and 'big bang' can work. The choice depends on our own personal situation, the people and the church's history. A new church plant or a church with no history of small groups may indeed be ideal for the prototype. What we need to do is to weigh the principles and apply them carefully to our own unique situation.

Proposing a strategy

Whichever route is adopted, the church has to come to a point where the whole package is taken on board. As one leader put it, 'Either you're pregnant or you're not pregnant!' If you are, the whole vision is going to grow in a measurable way until it inevitably comes to birth. When I returned from my first Cell Conference, I was definitely 'pregnant'. First, however, I needed to gather the church and assess to what extent we now shared the same values and could embrace the same vision. The process of consulting and sharing with the leadership took a couple of months, and then the decision was made to share it with the whole church. Over several evenings, the vision was presented and explained and every small group was invited to discuss it and feed back questions and concerns. Those concerns were addressed at more meetings until there was a consensus to move forward. At that point we closed down the existing home groups and came together as a whole fellowship for two months during Lent. This period was used for teaching and training and corporate prayer, smoothing off the rough edges of our vision and encouraging others on board.

Presenting the plan

Communication can be tricky at the best of times, but never more so than when major change is in the air. At these times, it's often not what we say but the way we say it that is all-important. On one level, the transition to a cell-based model has profound implications for the way we do church. If we opt for the whole package, we'll never be the same again. But on another level, once a church is embracing the values, its development towards cell is a logical and practical step by step process.

When a church is considering the 'big bang', for instance, four points can be made about the transition of existing small groups. First, in one sense they shouldn't feel radically different, because the values we already hold dear will be employed in greater measure. That, of course, will mean a greater commitment to discipling, community, evangelism and prayer, but it will also mean greater support and encouragement too. So they may not be radically different, but they will be radically developed.

Second, they needn't necessarily be revolutionized, but they will be reorganized. Once the vision has been cast and people are responding, different options will apply to different groups. Some groups will be completely new. Some will divide and multiply because they're already too large. And some will want to disband and have a totally fresh start. All the groups are simply asked to examine what they already have and ask some honest questions about their values and vision.

Third, it's good to assure people that cell groups won't be compulsory, but they will become a crucial part of our life together. Sunday worship is not compulsory, but you soon realize that you really miss out if you never come. Similarly, cell life will not be compulsory, but if it provides all the things that we're hoping for and expecting, then eventually you will miss out if you're not a part of it.

Fourth, they need not be set up in opposition to other ministries, but increasingly they will be integral to them. This means that we won't forcibly close an organization because of cell groups, but we will allow cells to become the number one priority in the life of the church. Inevitably some organizations and programmes will begin to lose their importance and will eventually dwindle and die. Some will agree to close now because the vision for cell has highlighted the need. Others will sharpen their focus so that they can integrate more closely with cell life. All the organizations will eventually exist to serve the cells and encourage their growth.

I believe those are the four main practical issues with which house groups will wrestle, but each one will have its own personal concerns, and they too need to be addressed.

Persuading the sceptics

Somebody once told me that in any process of change, ten per cent of the people will welcome it quickly and uncritically and a further ten per cent will reject it with equal fervour. The other 80 per cent will embrace it if the process is clearly explained and gently led. I don't know where the study was made, but it certainly rings true in my own experience. If a vision is Christ-centred and based on biblical values, and if it's open to scrutiny and correction, the majority of followers will unite around it. It's important to enable that process by removing any obstacles in people's way, taking time to explain the vision, reduce misunderstanding and dispel the fears.

Personally, I've found that question-and-answer evenings are an invaluable tool in clarifying the vision. People are invited to write down their questions and send them in anonymously if they wish. The questions arrive before the evening to allow time for proper reflection and preparation. Doing it this way has several advantages. First, it allows the leadership to give a considered response. Second, it eliminates the possibility of the meeting being hijacked by the more articulate who can easily dominate the discussion. And third, it assures the church that every question is deemed important and will be answered.

Occasionally, of course, the anonymous questioner will write something unhelpful or offensive, but even that can be used as a teaching tool about what we do and do not value in communication! It's in this context that many hidden agendas and fears can be addressed. Often, there's just one question in a person's mind that dominates their whole thinking, and until that question is addressed, they'll find it very difficult or impossible to hear anything else. However irrelevant, hostile or trivial the questions may seem, we need to value where people are coming from and meet them where they are.

As we meet them, there are five fears in particular that people tend to express about cell church.

It will burn out leaders

Whenever people say this, it's usually because they've taken hold of the headlines about cell and ignored the detail. They hear the assertion that every cell is authentically church, then apply a full-time staff model to the cell leader's role. If a cell is a church, that means that we're asking the leaders to be multi-gifted mini-vicars who can run their own little congregation. In fact, the opposite is true. Leadership is spread very widely and support is offered continuously. The cell leader is far less likely to burn out than the beleaguered self-reliant leader of a Bible study group.

It will leave out people

Here, the fear is that the more cell becomes the central focus in a church's life, the more people on the fringe will feel left out. However, the opposite tends to happen. First of all, most people who hover on the fringe often do so because that's where they want to be. They usually want to dip in and out without the commitment, and we tend to miss them far more than they miss us. In the cell structure, however, those people are adopted as part of the cell network. Without putting pressure on them, cell members will simply be there for those who are on the outside. Rather than ignore them, they will befriend them, pray for them and invite them to appropriate events. When they have a need, they no longer get lost in the crowd and left on the sidelines. The cell is aware and the concern can be met. In fact, at St Mark's, one of the most exciting results of transitioning has been to see the uninterested and uncommitted being slowly drawn in to the Christian community.

It will push out mission

The concern here is that our wider mission mandate is reduced to a narrow concern with evangelism and head counting. This, however, is where the five values together keep a healthy balance on our understanding of mission. To create genuine Christian community is to have a genuine involvement in the community as a whole and a concern for the poor, for justice and for a broken world in general. Mission in its widest sense is an integral part of cell life.

It will squeeze out spontaneity

The fear here is that cell church can easily give the impression of offering little more than a very rigid programme, a single narrow track that every Christian must be passed along. The idea possibly arises out of seeing countless diagrams drawn to describe the mechanics of cell. Certainly a strong structure is involved, and various tracks need to be considered in making the vision run smoothly. I hope I have now made the point that cell church is far more about life than structures. I would also want to say here that I've never yet seen or heard of a cell church that doesn't have its own unique personality. Although every cell-based church embraces every value and follows similar patterns, there is still a lot of room for spontaneous expression. Cell conferences will offer specific teaching and training materials, but there is no package.

It will drown out spirituality

As in any major new vision, the danger is that the vision itself becomes more important than the underlying values. Before we know it, the church can be talking far more about cell than about Jesus. John Wimber had a favourite saying when people were in danger of becoming obsessed with the latest vision or idea. He used to say, 'The main thing is to keep the main thing the main thing.' Fortunately that is a key value in the life of the cell church. As we concentrate on encountering God, we get powerful and consistent reminders that 'it's all about Jesus'.

Practising leadership

If it's right for your church to pursue this vision, then the role of the vicar or senior pastor is crucial. Sadly, I've met church leaders who think cell church is a very good idea, and then delegated its implementation to the curate or other assistant leader. Clearly, they've missed the whole point. They've reduced what they've read to yet another programme that'll boost the morale of ailing home groups. The result is tagging a few cell church principles on to what we already have and making a few improvements. The results may indeed appear encouraging at first, but the kind of fruit that we really need won't appear until all the values are applied and in place. Transition on this scale is going to lead to transformation, and something as significant as that needs the blessing and passion and leadership of the senior pastor. Let me suggest three leadership priorities that are essential during transition.

Model the values

You can never lead a person beyond where you are yourself, so before we check out the congregation's response, we have to examine our own hearts and motivation. Looking carefully through the five values, it would take a very shallow leader not to be challenged by one or two areas of weakness in themselves as well as in the church. To model these values is to begin making ourselves vulnerable and recognizing where the starting point is going to be at a personal level. Having done that, we have to refocus our whole ministry to put cell life at the centre. It will take courage to ask others to make cell groups a priority and perhaps find that they may have to drop other commitments that we rely on. We ourselves must be seen pruning our own diaries to make them a priority.

We also have to find practical ways of living out cell values as ministers and leaders. When we first began covenant cells, I became a member of two cells and tried to demonstrate what I was asking of people in terms of being accountable. At first it was quite a revelation for some people to discover that their vicar still struggled with prayer and Bible reading! Since then, I've been helping to establish a growing network of church leaders on a regional and national level, where we as clergy can learn to be accountable to our peers in terms of our leadership. Together, we've designed another card with a list of questions that apply to our own particular calling and role (see Appendix 5). In a safe and supportive place, we seek to be honest and real about our struggles and dreams, and have grown increasingly to love and appreciate these times.

Make the time

When I first read the job profile for a prospective new vicar at St Mark's, I was seriously tempted to think that they were looking for Jesus. Then I realized that he wouldn't have got the job because he wasn't married with two children! It was obvious that the church was committed to developing every-member ministry, but equally clear that they'd also like to retain the traditional vicar role. I took the job and spent several years trying to work through the tension of being all things to all people. Eventually, though, I came to accept that change had to start with me. Not only did I need the courage to confront the inevitable criticism of failing to live up to everyone's expectations, but I also needed to be far more ruthless in prioritizing time and modelling what was required. That meant that I needed to stop doing a few good things in order to make time for the 'God' thing that I was called to do.

Mark 1 became a very helpful anchor passage in making the change. It paints an amazing picture of the pressure on Jesus as 'the whole town gathered at the door' for healing (v. 33). We see Jesus retreating to pray and Simon Peter looking for him. When he finds him, you can hear the note of reproach in his voice: 'Everyone is looking for you' (v. 37). Clearly he'd only healed 'many' in the village and by no means all of them. Imagine the pressure on Jesus to go and heal more people. Amazingly he replies, 'Let's go somewhere else—to the nearby villages—so that I can preach there also. That is why I have come' (v. 38). As I read that I can imagine how one or two followers could have replied, 'A lot of people are going to feel let down, Lord. We understand of course, but I'm not sure if they will. Still, if you just want to preach…' I'd have caved in immediately but Jesus had prayed about his priorities and organized his life and his time with great confidence, knowing that his Father approved of what he was doing. Jesus was called to move towards Jerusalem and the cross, where he'd achieve a far greater healing for the whole human race. Every chapter of Mark describes how Jesus 'left there', 'withdrew', 'went on', 'went up', 'went across', 'went around', 'came to another place'. One of the key characteristics of leadership is to hear God's call on our lives, and not to be distracted from following it. A vision for cell church is a vision for the whole church and for the whole of our ministry. It's impossible to implement that vision without making the space to follow it through. We have to make the time.

Mentor your leaders

Books like this can begin to impart vision and offer specific guidance, but real learning in the kingdom of God is a relational process. We need one another—to address the blind spots and deal with the weaknesses—and we need large and constant amounts of collective wisdom on a one-to-one level. The more we've pursued this vision in our church, the more questions have been raised along the way. The questions have nothing to do with the values or overall strategy, but with the practical, down-to-earth details that confront us every day. I now spend hours with my leaders sorting through specific problems in the vision and wrestling with possible solutions. Again and again we come back to the same answers, but we need reminding of them over and over again, and we need each other's encouragement and support in implementing them. That's why cell churches take training and appraisal seriously, knowing that it takes very little to begin diluting these values. What we don't need is another committee meeting. When leaders gather, the very principles they value and teach about should be flowing through the group itself. A leadership team that puts accountability, community and encounter at the top of its own agenda can expect it to appear in the rest of the fellowship far faster as the vision spreads. It also means that we don't just meet. We build our friendships, open our homes and make it all a lot more fun!

Producing a transformation

Jesus never did things by halves. By the time he'd finished in Cana, there were six waterpots containing vintage wine. Since each one held between 20 and 30 gallons, that means that there could have been up to 180 gallons of wine flowing at that reception—rather more than several receptions might need! 'Abundance' is a key word in God's kingdom. Whenever we are in need, we will find more than enough, especially when we are facing the challenge of transformation in the church. Whatever God is calling you to do in your church, the combination of his grace and your obedience will produce new wine. The two key questions are: what is he asking you to do, and will you do it? The Cana story has a very simple message, and it comes on the lips of Mary when she says, 'Do whatever he tells you' (v. 5). The last impression I want to give in these chapters is that your church must be celled and celled now. The important thing is for us to share our blessing and offer it to others and then stand back. The vital thing for you is simply to weigh the possibilities then 'do whatever he tells you'.

Cell outline

Welcome

Can you think of a memorable moment from a wedding you have attended—amusing, embarrassing, moving? (It might even be your own!)

Worship

'The main thing is to keep the main thing the main thing!'

Focus on Jesus as the Bridegroom and us as his Bride. Play a song that speaks about our love relationship with Jesus, inviting people to reflect on the intimacy and passion of God's love, then read out one or two of the following passages and respond to them in prayer and praise:

- Song of Songs 2:16–17; 3:1–5
- Hosea 2:14–23
- Revelation 19:5–9

Pray that your vision as a church will always be centred on Jesus and your love for him.

Word

Use the time to begin to assess how far the vision of cell church is right for your group and your church at this time. Use the following headings as a guide.

- **Pursuing the vision:** Do you feel in principle that this is a vision you want to embrace?
- **Preparing the ground:** To what extent do you feel that the five core values are already in place? What may need more attention before going any further?

- **Planning the transition:** How do you respond to the two main options of 'prototype' and 'big bang'?
- **Proposing a strategy:** If this vision is right for you, what kind of timescale would you like to see operating?
- **Presenting the plan:** What are the key areas and concerns you would need to focus on and address?
- **Persuading the sceptics:** How do you envisage the other groups in your church responding? Where may patience, wisdom and sensitivity be needed?
- **Practising leadership:** If you could say one key thing about this to your vicar or senior pastor, what would it be?
- **Producing a transformation:** Gather all the points of your discussion together, lay aside your own concerns and preferences, and ask the question, 'What is God saying to us in all this?'

Witness

Pray through the responses you have made, and pray especially for the leadership of your church and those who make the major decisions. Thank God for them and ask for a special anointing of the Holy Spirit on their lives as they consider the way ahead. Pray for your unity and the quality of your communication at this stage. Feed back your thoughts to the leadership.

Chapter 9

Bringing it Home

Jesus left there and went to his home town, accompanied by his disciples. When the Sabbath came, he began to teach in the synagogue, and many who heard him were amazed. 'Where did this man get these things?' they asked. 'What's this wisdom that has been given him, that he even does miracles! Isn't this the carpenter? Isn't this Mary's son and the brother of James, Joses, Judas and Simon? Aren't his sisters here with us?' And they took offence at him. Jesus said to them, 'Only in his home town, among his relatives and in his own house is a prophet without honour.' He could not do any miracles there, except lay his hands on a few sick people and heal them. And he was amazed at their lack of faith.

MARK 6:1–6

Have you ever noticed how this passage stands out like a very sore thumb in the Gospels? In the previous chapter we see the deliverance of Legion, the woman who touched Jesus' cloak and the raising of Jairus' daughter, three miracles. Immediately after we see the disciples driving out demons, the feeding of the five thousand and Jesus walking on water. But in the middle of it all, in his own home town, 'he could not do any miracles'. It's an amazing thought that despite all his authority and power, the Son of God could enter a place where the atmosphere was so sour and full of unbelief that he could not do the miracles he was performing everywhere else. Even Jesus was 'amazed at their lack of faith' (v. 6). I often come back to this passage and reflect on its warning against complacency and ignorance. In particular, it was the familiarity factor that became a faith killer: 'Isn't this the carpenter? Isn't this Mary's son?' (v. 3). In effect they were saying, 'This is not the Jesus we know and expect. We know him as a carpenter and we knew him as a child. He's played with us and worked with us, but he's never done anything like this before.' They were offended at the very thought of him being anything other than the man they already knew.

Unfortunately, you and I can fall into the same trap. We can be so wrapped up in the Jesus we know so far in our experience that familiarity, if it doesn't breed contempt, can certainly breed complacency. In some ways, the danger is greater for those who've known Jesus longer. Not only have we tasted his grace in our own lives, but we've seen it at work in our churches and our ministries. Indeed, we may have seen it especially in our home groups. So why would we ever want to consider replacing the blessing we've known and tasted with something we've never experienced? I think we all wrestle at times with a similar attitude to the Nazarenes, but if we're going to receive fresh vision and enter new ventures we need the humility to see that we'll always have more to discover. Even Paul, with his brilliant, incisive mind, was consumed with a desire to 'know how wide and long and high and deep is the love of Christ, and to know this love that surpasses knowledge' (Ephesians 3:19). And look at the apostle John. If ever anybody had a claim on knowing Jesus, it was him. Not only was he one of the twelve but one of the three, and the one that Jesus loved. Nobody knew Jesus better than John, but one day he was worshipping on the island of Patmos and he saw Christ again. He'd seen the human, healing, crucified and risen Christ. Now he saw the glorified Christ, whose 'head and hair were white like wool, as white as snow, and his eyes were like blazing fire' (Revelation 1:14). When he saw this Christ John 'fell at his feet as though dead' (v. 17). After this he saw Jesus drawing back the curtain of history to reveal his authority and sovereignty and a thousand more things than he'd never seen before.

Whenever new developments take place, we have a natural tendency to resist and question what more it can offer to what we already have. In terms of theology and spiritual understanding, there's nothing new about cell church. But very often the issue is more to do with heart knowledge than head knowledge. We can believe in something and think that we're doing it, when in fact we've missed the point or lost the plot along the way. What cell church has done for my own ministry is to help me become more honest and accountable in doing what I already believe in and love doing. My aim in writing this is to help you do the same—to examine the familiar and then hear God afresh. In doing that, we open ourselves to the possibility of further miracles, new insights that give us a fresh revelation of what it means to be church. For me, the miracle of cell has had nothing to do with dramatic events, but it's the growth and multiplication of little testimonies that add up to a major new move of God. That's why I want to finish this book at the heart of cell, in the lives of the 'little people' who are making it work. The following testimonies are just a few examples of what it means in the context of cell to have all involved, becoming disciples, creating community, doing evangelism and encountering God.

From some of the smaller 'little people'
(12–13 year olds)

'What I've valued in my cell group is...'

- 'It's different from church. I's easy to tell others about problems and know it won't go any further.'
- 'Talking in smaller groups means we all get a chance to say something. It's a comfy environment.'
- 'Getting closer, having a little family, having support around you. Friendships are strong, and it's good to know there are others like you who can help and understand.'
- 'People that I can trust. I can share everything and know people will help me.'

From one of our youth cells

'Since becoming a Christian this summer I've started going to cell on Monday nights. I didn't even know what 'cell' was so it's all pretty new to me. I like the way that everyone can get involved. For example, I prayed in the group. I found this very difficult. I think that this was difficult because I was worried about what I was going to say. Even though this is a small thing I feel like God really helped me.

'I went to cell on the first week and I happened to mention that I wanted to start reading the Bible. Dan (the leader) gave me a little booklet that got me started and I was totally shocked because I got so much out of it. I never thought the Bible would be interesting!

'I really do think I can trust the people in cell with anything I say. That's really important to me because I always have *a lot* to say. Seriously, I am thankful that I can talk everything through without feeling like I'm being judged or looked down on.

'For me, cell is important because I get to meet up with other Christians and have a lot of fun. Most of all, though, it's being around other Christians. It's really difficult at school or just with my friends to be a Christian. Cell really helps me because I'm able to talk to others who understand where I am coming from. Anyway, our cell is top!

From a new disciple

'I became a member of a cell about four months ago, having accepted Jesus into my life.

'Initially I was unsure and nervous about going into a cell. But despite this I still felt that I both wanted and needed to be in one. At that stage I didn't really know why, other than I had some vague thoughts about wanting to continue to learn and to meet with the group of people I already knew. At that early stage I really had no idea what I had let myself in for as a Christian.

'The first few weeks of cell were "tentative" as we all got to know each other more, got over our nerves and started to share things honestly (but even from the first I was hooked!). Gradually I found I couldn't bear to miss a meeting. There was a sort of mixture of need, excitement and hunger to learn more... the cell night was fast becoming the focus of my week. I was enjoying the company of the people in the cell. Unlike many other groups I had been in, these were nice people who really cared about each other and about me.

'As we discussed things in the cell and as we helped each other I gradually came to realize that while I had made a big step in becoming a Christian, it was only the first step. I have begun to understand that there is so much more to my life in following Jesus than just being forgiven. This is such a daunting and yet exciting prospect. It's only through cell that I have had a chance to receive the support of others who understand all that I face and can offer support and guidance. In the cell I feel I can talk freely about my walk with Jesus and continue to learn and grow.

'I thank God that by his grace he has brought me to this spot and that he draws me back to the group each week.'

From a married couple

'A friend invited us to his house for a meeting (it was a cell group meeting) and reluctantly we went along. We were both touched by the love coming from people we didn't know and we both felt immediately at ease. When members of the cell offered to pray for us we also felt the love of God and the cleansing power of the Holy Spirit touching us. We found we were able to ask many questions about Christ, in what we felt was a safe environment, and no question was considered too silly.

'Over the weeks we received much encouragement, guidance and prayer and this eventually led us to attend St Mark's on Sundays as well. We haven't looked back since.

'Twelve months on we began leading a cell ourselves and it has gone full circle as through God's grace, we are now helping other 'new' Christians.'

From a policeman

'As a police officer I lived a very selfish life. I drank too much, was always the centre of attention, and money and fast living were my gods. Throughout this time, apart from my involvement as a freemason, commitment was a word I avoided strongly.

'Three years ago I did an Alpha course, then joined a cell with some of my colleagues. The cell showed me genuine love. The pastoral care of the leader showed me the meaning of self-worth, something I hadn't known before. After two years I became a cell leader and the Lord has increasingly been showing me the meaning of obedience and accountability. Evangelism has also taken on a totally new meaning for me and is now increasingly a natural extension of my life. I am now far more centred on Christ. I hunger for more of him constantly in my own life and in the lives of the people I love.'

From one of our less confident members

'I joined a cell group, the whole church was joining a cell group! I didn't want to miss out. In time the group bonded and I felt part of a "family". I was the quiet one in the corner, taking everything in but not contributing too much. Step by step I was asked to do a little something for the group, say a reading, choose some music. This made me feel more involved and gave me confidence. I was asked to consider being a co-leader in my group and this, to be honest, filled me with fear! "I can't do that, I don't know enough, etc." But with the help of a supportive and encouraging cell leader I did become cell co-leader.

'I was happy to assist, but I relied on her a lot for my confidence. She was such a great encourager and I began to believe that maybe I could be a decent co-leader, but only with her help. However just as I was settling into my comfort zone, my cell pastor and cell leader asked whether I would be willing to take on our original cell as cell leader as the present leader was being asked to begin a new cell with members from a recent Alpha course. It was at this time I had to stop relying on my cell leader for my support and start relying on the Lord. I really didn't want to take it on and make a mess of it all, but I now know the Lord can take weak people and begin to do things through them. He has honoured and blessed the step I took for him. Our cell group continues to grow and each member has continued to open and blossom. It is such a privilege to watch the Lord at work.'

From one who'd lost her way

'I had belonged to a cell for about eighteen months and it was a really important part of my church life and my walk with God. Then I sinned "big time". I really hurt God, my family, myself and many other people.

'I repented many, many times to God with tears and a very heavy heart. It took months, but I went to see my cell leaders, Tony and Chris, expecting them to say I couldn't ever go to the cell again. Instead they listened and prayed for me and over the next few months they just loved and supported me and my husband.

'I was welcomed into the cell and allowed to heal and grow with God. The sin wasn't played down but the love was stepped up. I stayed with the group and two-and-a-half years down the road I'm now a co-leader.

'By God's grace and the love of that cell, my joy and confidence have returned.'

They returned with joy

Not long after that depressing day in Nazareth, Jesus started to send out his imperfect little team of disciples from village to village (Mark 6:6–13), and eventually, as the ministry increased, 72 of them 'returned with joy' (Luke 10:17). Who knows how strange it had felt when they first stepped out in faith? But they'd also seen and received enough from Jesus to be confident and expectant. I suspect too, that Nazareth had given them a stark reminder of the empty alternative when it comes to faith. However they were feeling, they'd gone out with the cell church motto that 'God's strength shows up best in weak people'. That's what thrilled Jesus and it still delights him now. My prayer is that however we do church, we will learn to do it his way, in a way that brings him joy. 'At that time, Jesus, full of joy through the Holy Spirit, said, 'I praise you, Father, Lord of heaven and earth, because you have hidden these things from the wise and learned, and revealed them to little children. Yes, Father, for this was your good pleasure' (Luke 10: 21).

That, for me, sums up the miracle of cells!

Cell outline

Welcome

When did you last take a risk and what was the outcome? (Something you bought, someone you helped, a job or a project you took on, a place you decided to visit, or whatever.)

Worship

Read together Revelation 1:12–19.

Reflect quietly on the message to the seven churches in chapters 2 and 3. Respond to what you have read in worship, focusing on Jesus:

- His character, and the endless and awesome revelation he brings into our lives.
- His faithfulness, and all the ways he has blessed and answered our prayers so far.
- His conviction in areas we (like the seven churches) need to repent about.
- His blessing on our desire to love him more.

Word

Read together Luke 10:17–24.

- As you have considered together the challenge of cell church, what in particular has made you feel like 'little children', conscious of your weakness but his strength?
- Where will you need his strength as a group and as a church as you go forward into the future?
- Whether or not you become a cell-based church, what do you feel will bring Jesus 'joy' as you respond to him now? What is he asking you to do above anything else?

Witness

Do you have a fresh vision for your witness as a group? How has God been speaking to you about reaching out to others? What are your immediate goals in this area? Pray them through together.

Chapter 10

Putting it Another Way...

Over the past three years, one of our cell pastors has chronicled our progress into cell with scores of cartoons. Ron Bailey's humour has really captured the essence of our transition, the learning curves and the many smiles and tears along the way. Anyone who embarks on the road to cell church will make many mistakes. Our advice at St Mark's is not only to learn from them, but to laugh as well—we're pretty sure the Lord does! So here's a small sample to summarize the message of this book.

Cell is all about approaching Church in a whole new way...

THERE WAS NO MISTAKING THE CELL CHURCH IN SOME STREETS.

It's all about helping people belong...

....AND SO I LEFT MY
PREVIOUS CELL GROUP BECAUSE
I FOUND PEOPLE DIDN'T TAKE
ENOUGH NOTICE OF ME....

It's about helping people into greater commitment...

NO, I'M SORRY, WE CAN'T COME
FOR AN ALL PAID FOR SLAP UP MEAL,
FOLLOWED BY BEST SEATS
IN THE THEATRE - WE'VE
GOT TO LEAD A
CELL MEETING

It's about encouraging more people into ministry and leadership...

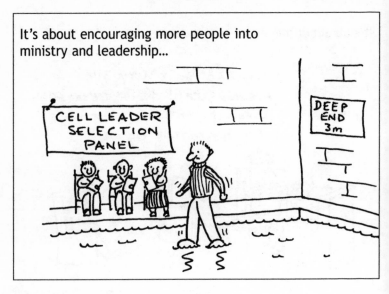

It's about training, encouraging and walking alongside people...

It's about learning to be sensitive in evangelism...

Learning to be real and honest with each other...

It's about quality of fellowship...

SOME LEADERS' STRENGTHS LAY IN
PREPARING FOR THE AFTER CELL SNACK TIME.

Quality of welcome...

Quality of worship...

SOME LEADERS' ATTEMPTS TO ACCOMPANY
WORSHIP WERE TO BE ADMIRED

Quality of learning...

I DON'T KNOW HOW YOU MANAGE TO
DO YOUR PREPARATION BETWEEN
THE END OF 'CORONATION STREET'
AND THE GROUP ARRIVING AT EIGHT

Quality of prayer...

Quality of care...

So there's nothing strange and alien about cell church—
it's all perfectly normal and really worth looking at!

THE LATEST THEME PARKS
GAVE VISITORS THE CHANCE TO SEE
REAL LIVE CELL GROUPS

Cell Health Check

The following list is used by the cell pastor to help the cell leader reflect on the life and health of their cell. The aim is to set aside an hour or so about three times a year to do this. The questions are simply a guide for the cell pastors to help them home in on any currently important issues.

Personal

1. What do you think of it all so far?
2. Are you enjoying it?
   - All of the time
   - Most of the time
   - Some of the time
   - None of the time
3. In what ways do you feel it has:
   - encouraged you?
   - stretched you?
   - challenged you?
4. Have you found the cell pastor role helpful in any way?
5. Is there anything more we can do to help you?

Communication and community

1. How accountable and thoughtful are all the members to the needs and life of the group?
   - How often do they come?
   - Do they let you know when they can't?
   - Do they offer help?
   - Do they offer homes?
2. How often do you talk to each cell member outside the meeting? Are you making weekly contact?

3. How many cell members have you been able to spend quality time with since the cell started?
4. Are there any things you find difficult about this?
5. Do you manage to pray regularly for each cell member?

Welcome/Gathering

1. Do you find it easy to start and end on time?
2. How much time do you spend on this on average?
3. How often do you use an icebreaker?
   • Weekly
   • Fortnightly
   • Monthly
   • Other
4. How many others are involved in leading this section?

Worship/Glorifying

1. Overall, do you feel a sense of 'breaking through into God's presence' or not?
2. What do you find most difficult?
3. What works best?
4. How much time do you spend in worship?
5. How many others are involved in leading this section?

Word/Growing

1. How helpful do you find the material?
2. Do you find the questions relevant to people's situations?
3. How often does this section lead into a ministry time?
4. What do you find most difficult in leading this section of the meeting?
5. Does anyone else share the leadership of this section with you?

Witness/Going

1. Describe how you're using this section to 'send people out'.
2. How long do you spend on this?
3. How many of the cell get involved in prayer and ministry?

Evangelism in the Cell

1. Do you feel the cell has a healthy awareness of the fundamental aim of the cell (to grow and multiply)?
2. How often do you pray specifically for the people on the cell members' *oikos* list?
3. What evangelistic/bridge building/social events have you had recently? Which ones have worked well?
4. How many new members have been added to the group?
5. Are these:
   - Established church members
   - 'Fringe' or irregular members
   - Transferred from another church
   - New Christians
6. Is anyone being approached to attend the next Alpha course? (Names and details please.)

Any other comments

By sharing insights with each other, we can help our cells to grow and multiply.

Please share anything:
- you are finding particularly difficult
- you have found particularly encouraging
- you feel we need to address in teaching and training and so on.

Prayer Points

Are there three or four particular things that you would like to focus on for development over the next few months? Share them and name them so that we can pray for these together.

50 Icebreakers

'Getting to know you': Facts

- What is your most satisfying accomplishment ever?
- What is your happiest memory?
- Describe the most significant event in your life.
- Who has most changed your life?
- What do you find most boring and unenjoyable about your work?
- What do you enjoy most about it?
- What is your favourite food?
- Describe yourself in four words.
- What was the best advice you have ever received?
- Describe one of the happiest days of your life.
- What ability do you possess that you like most?
- What's the longest phone conversation you have ever had and with whom were you speaking?
- What was your favourite toy as a child?
- What animal best describes your personality?
- If you could ask Noah a question, what would it be?
- Use a colour to describe your week and tell us why you chose that colour.
- When you were sick as a child, what was the best thing your parents did to make you feel better?
- What was your favourite subject at school?
- Did you ever have a favourite outfit (clothes) that others thought was ugly?
- As a child, who was your favourite babysitter?
- Name a vehicle which best describes yourself. Explain why you chose this vehicle.
- If you could use a symbol to describe yourself, what would it be?

- What are your favourite clothes? (Head to toe.)
- Mime something that describes you or something you enjoy doing.
- Describe something you find difficult to do.
- Tell of something that has made you laugh/smile during this last week.

'Getting to know you': Interests

- What kind of social gathering or party do you like best? (For example, pub, sport, leisure, club, and so on.)
- What is your favourite radio or TV programme?
- Name three kinds of work you would like to do.
- What do you like best about church?
- What do you most enjoy doing in your spare time?
- What is your favourite time of day?
- What are three of your favourite activities?
- If you could spend the day with a celebrity, who would it be?
- You have just been selected captain of your team. What sport would it be?

'Getting to know you': Values

- Draw your own coat of arms as you would like it to be (to best describe you), and explain it to the group.
- What would you most like to be or do for the next five years, if there were no limitations of family, money, education, health and so on?
- What present would you most like to receive?
- Where would you live if you could, and what would you do there?
- What kind of things make you irritated or furious?
- What makes you feel anxious or afraid?
- Describe one of your goals in life.
- If you had to move and could only take three things, what would they be?
- If you were given a large amount of money, what would be the first thing you would do with it?

- If you could spend the rest of your life doing exactly what you wanted, what would you do?
- If you were shipwrecked on a deserted island, what one tool would you want to have with you?
- If you only had one way to communicate, would you choose the computer, sign language, or singing?
- If you could have anything you want for your birthday dinner, what would it be? (Keep in mind that the meal is free and you won't gain weight!)
- If money was no object, what kind of party would you throw for your friends?
- Draw a picture of yourself doing something you enjoy. (Fold the pictures in half, place in the centre of the group and get everyone to choose one piece of folded paper and then try to guess who it is and what they are doing.)

50 Suggestions for Social Evenings

These were brainstormed by the cells themselves, and many could be very suitable to invite friends and neighbours in order to show them that Christians are 'normal' people.

Meals
- Barbecue
- Fondue evening
- Picnic
- Chip butty night
- Bring and share supper
- Dinner party
- Food theme night (for example, Chinese, Italian, Indian, and so on)
- Harvest supper
- Christmas dinner
- Progressive dinner (Starter at one house, main at next, sweet at another, finishing with coffee and mints at the last house. Variations can be made. For example, you can go to each other's houses and just have a drink or whatever)
- Hot-pot supper (A Lancashire dish of stew, potatoes and carrots topped with a crust) You can extend this by dressing up in old Lancashire-style clothes and singing Lancashire songs!
- Cheese and wine evening

Home-based
- Quiz night
- Games evening (for example, board games such as Trivial Pursuit, Scrabble, Monopoly, Balderdash—or dominoes)
- Video and drinks
- Beauty for Ashes (make-up and beauty care demonstration)

- Craft evening (where you could invite others and give the proceeds to charity)
- Bring and buy (where you could invite others and give the proceeds to charity)
- Invite another cell group to join you for the evening
- Generation game (your own interpretation of the TV quiz show but using cell members and guests instead of family connections)
- Talent show
- Celebrity guest evening
- Desert Island Discs (where each member plays a favourite piece of music and explains why they've chosen it)
- Party
- Fancy dress evening
- Murder mystery evening (invite another cell)

Active
- Treasure hunt (walking or driving)
- Ten-pin bowling
- Cycle ride
- Carol singing
- Barn dance
- Swimming
- After-service walk/picnic
- 1960s/1970s/1980s evening (focusing on the music and dress of the particular decade you choose)
- Gardening/decorating evening (or another practical need)
- Day out at a theme park, circus or zoo
- Community visit (for example, open day at the local fire station)
- Evenings out
- Movie/pizza
- Football or rugby match
- Theatre, pantomime, concert or cinema
- Car rally
- Inter-cell games evening
- Carpet bowls

- Pub
- Event at church (for example, special outreach evening)
- Bonfire party
- Evening cell shop (visit your local shopping centre)
- Roller skating, ice skating, Laser Quest, paintball evening
- Pot auction (bring items like ornaments and household goods to put up for auction, the money raised to go to a charity of your choice)

50 Suggestions for Prayer Evenings

There are many ways of praying, and varying forms can be appropriate at different times. This particular list was compiled by the cells themselves. Many of the ideas are obvious, but the purpose was to brainstorm them and remind each other of the wealth of resources at our disposal.

Meditations

1. Choose a picture as a visual aid (for example a country scene). Meditate on the picture and use it:
    *   To ask God to show you something of himself in it
    *   As a focus for worship
    *   As a means of discerning what God is saying to you personally.
2. Have a basket full of different kinds of stone, rough and smooth. Ask members of the cell to choose a stone and, as they feel it, allow God to speak to them about themselves or about him. Alternatively, have a basket of coloured stones and ask members to choose one that reminds them of the personality of a person they know (or even a member of the group), then pray for that person.
3. Candles
4. Meditate on a piece of music, one that lends itself to this either because of the words, an evocative tune, or a particular theme.
5. Close your eyes and imagine Jesus is in front of you. What would you say to him and what does he say to you?
6. Meditation on an object (for example, a cross)
7. Take a passage from the gospels and imagine that you are there. What is it like (weather, people and so on)? What is Jesus like; what is he saying; what does it mean to you?
8. Spend an evening in silence: you can use Bibles, favourite objects from home or other items to help you meditate on God.

9. Dirty rocks: handle them and then wash your hands to symbolize forgiveness.
10. Pre-written prayers put around the room to pray through and think about.

Structured prayer

1. Pray the psalms (for example, as if they were from you).
2. Books of prayers (for example, Bible, liturgy, hymns, other prayer books).
3. Complete the sentences: 'Lord, thank you…'; 'Lord, you are…'
4. Choose a prayer from the psalms and discuss how the original author felt when writing it.
5. Choose a hymn, discuss and pray around it.
6. Take a short passage of scripture, read and pray through each verse.
7. Read a passage of scripture aloud leaving space between verses to think about it.
8. Use the Lord's Prayer as a focus and structure for your own prayers.
9. ACTS—Adoration, Confession, Thanksgiving, Supplication. Move around the group with different people doing the different parts.
10. Write prayers and read them out.
11. 'Saints at Prayer'—a six-week Anglican Renewal Ministries course (available from ARM).
12. Ask members to bring written prayers to read aloud.
13. Write topics for prayer on a handful of ping-pong balls, then choose a ball and pray for that topic.
14. Write repentance prayers down on bits of paper and then burn them.

General group prayer

1. Prayer triplets: break up into threes and pray for each other. Pray through any problems. This can be carried on outside the cell meeting weekly or monthly.

2.   Prayer chain (telephone): each member to have a list of names and telephone numbers of everyone in the cell. When a prayer request or emergency arises, the leader contacts the first person on the list, who then contacts the second, and so on. This is a fast and efficient way of getting a lot of people praying in a short space of time.

3.   Prayer basket: members of the cell place a prayer request in a basket. Each member then picks one out and reads the prayer out loud, then takes it home with them and prays it through for the rest of the week.

4.   Prayer diary: ask one or two members to take responsibility for the diary. Write any prayer items in the diary along with the date entered. As you pray them through over the weeks, enter into the diary any answers and in what ways they've been answered.

5.   Prayer poems: use poems to meditate on in prayer or try as a group or individually to write a poem then use it in prayer.

6.   Ask members of the group to say one-line prayers.

7.   Pool prayer points and invite each individual to pray for one point.

8.   Pray in pairs.

9.   Prayer breakfast: meet up before work to pray together and share a simple breakfast.

10. Whole-night or half-night of prayer.

11. Theme night: choose two or three very specific topics and concentrate solely on these (world disaster, church needs, organizations, ministries, the sick). Saturate them in prayer from all angles.

12. Pray out loud all at once.

13. Pray for the person on your left/right in the cell meeting.

Intercessory prayer

1.   Walk to a spot overlooking your area, and pray for your village/town/city.

2.   Look together at a map of your area. Pray for the streets where you live and whatever happens nearby (for example, schools, shops, places of work).

3. Prayer walk: identify a couple of streets or a particular area in your locality. Walk round that area praying quietly for it. Pray for the people living in the houses and any public buildings you pass (schools, pubs, shops).

4. Prayer visiting: if you are aware of anyone in need of specific prayer, offer to go as a group and pray for them.

5. Pray as a group for one family member.

6. Pray through issues raised in the newspapers: bring cuttings to the meeting.

7. Prayer wall: have two lists—a list of prayer requests which are moved to the other list when answered. ('No' is an answer!)

8. Use different corners of the room as a focus for different subjects for prayer. Spend five or ten minutes in each corner praying for each subject. Each person can choose their own order of corners.

9. Fast for the day before having your cell evening. You could end the meeting itself with some food.

Praise

1. Thanksgiving/praise evening: concentrate on all that God has done for you and given you as a group and individually, then praise him in prayer and worship.

2. Half the group pray prayers of intercession while the other praises, then swap around.

3. Each member of the cell praises God for something that he has done for them in the last week (no matter how small it may seem).

4. Praise God for his creation: concentrate on the world around us—flowers, trees, mountains, sea, new birth. Maybe use visuals such as fresh flowers, pictures, postcards, holiday photographs.

Final thing

If all else fails, invite the vicar to spend an evening with you!

Church Leaders' Covenant Questions

Search me, O God, and know my heart.
PSALM 139:23

- Am I leading with a servant heart?
- Do I model what I teach?
- Am I teachable and accountable?
- Am I available and approachable?
- Do I listen well?
- Do I make myself vulnerable to others?
- Do I keep my promises?
- Do I give in to pressure?
- Do I make enough space for prayer?
- Do I keep my perspective?
- Do I still have a passion?
- Do I preach for a response?
- Do I still feel his pleasure?
- Do I study the Bible for me?
- Do I manage my time well?
- Am I taking enough rest?
- Is my family happy?
- Do I love the flock?
- Am I mentoring my leaders?
- Am I ministering grace?
- Am I walking with integrity?
- Am I living in the power of the Spirit?
- Am I keeping my cutting edge?
- Am I decisive and confident?
- Am I willing to take risks?
- Am I setting goals and reaching them?
- Am I willing to make sacrifices?
- Do I still have a vision for my church?
- Is my church growing in every sense?

Notes

1. Philip Yancey and Dr Paul Brand, *Fearfully and Wonderfully Made*, Hodder & Stoughton, 1981, p. 15.

2. Dr David (Paul) Yonggi Cho, *Successful Home Cell Groups*, Bridge Publishing, 1981.

3. Howard Astin, *Body & Cell*, Monarch Books, 1998.

4. Ralph Neighbour Jnr., *Where Do We Go From Here?* Touch Publications, 1990.

5. Bill Beckham, *The Second Reformation*, Touch Publications, 1993, p. 25.

6. David Watson, *I Believe in Evangelism*, Hodder & Stoughton, 1976, p. 57.

7. Howard A. Snyder, *The Radical Wesley and Patterns for Church Renewal*, InterVarsity Press, 1980, p. 59.

8. Dietrich Bonhoeffer, *Life Together*, Harper and Row, 1976, pp. 15–17.

9. Rick Warren, *The Purpose-Driven Church*, Zondervan, 1995.

10. C.S. Lewis, *The Problem of Pain*, Collins, 1940, p. 81.

11. Michael Harper, *A New Way of Living*, Hodder & Stoughton, 1973, p. 123.

12. William Barclay, *The Gospel of John*, Saint Andrew Press, Edinburgh, 1972, p. 155.

CPAS

Church Pastoral Aid Society

CPAS is an Anglican mission agency working across the United Kingdom and the Republic of Ireland, providing a wealth of resources for leaders of local churches. These include consultancy, training and publications.

For general information about the Society, please use the contact information below.

For guidance on cell church issues, and information about our cell church resources, please contact CPAS Regional Consultant Tony Hardy. Tel: (01744) 454303 E-mail: thardy@cpas.org.uk

The Church Pastoral Aid Society
Athena Drive
Tachbrook Park
WARWICK
CV34 6NG

Tel: (01926) 458458
E-mail: mail@cpas.org.uk
Web: www.cpas.org.uk

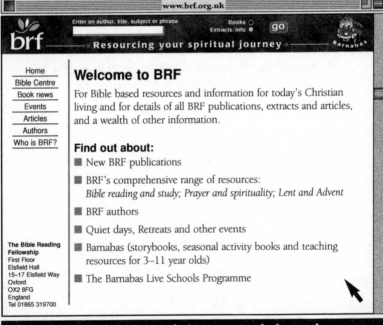

www.brf.org.uk

Enter an author, title, subject or phrase

Books ○
Extracts/Info ●

go

brf ——— Resourcing your spiritual journey ———

Home
Bible Centre
Book news
Events
Articles
Authors
Who is BRF?

Welcome to BRF

For Bible based resources and information for today's Christian living and for details of all BRF publications, extracts and articles, and a wealth of other information.

Find out about:

- New BRF publications

- BRF's comprehensive range of resources:
  Bible reading and study; Prayer and spirituality; Lent and Advent

- BRF authors

- Quiet days, Retreats and other events

- Barnabas (storybooks, seasonal activity books and teaching resources for 3–11 year olds)

- The Barnabas Live Schools Programme

The Bible Reading Fellowship
First Floor
Elsfield Hall
15–17 Elsfield Way
Oxford
OX2 8FG
England
Tel 01865 319700

Visit the BRF website at www.brf.org.uk

BRF is a Registered Charity

Visit the website of St Mark's Haydock at **www.stmarkshaydock.org**